P9-BAW-060

Leadership for Volunteering

Leadership
for
Volunteering

by Harriet H. Naylor

DRYDEN ASSOCIATES
DRYDEN, NEW YORK

DEDICATION

To the nicest people in the world,
the volunteers I have known, and
the professionals who have made
that possible.

LEADERSHIP FOR VOLUNTEERING

Copyright © 1976 by
Dryden Associates

All rights reserved.
No part of this book may be reproduced in any form
without permission in writing from the publisher.
Inquiries should be addressed to Dryden Associates
Box 363, Dryden, New York 13053

Library of Congress catalog card number: 76-49735

PRINTED IN THE UNITED STATES OF AMERICA

361.37
N333l

Contents

40226

FOREWORD

Like the number of volunteers, the number of people who help them to choose how to work and who undergird their efforts has grown tremendously in the past few years. As predicted in VOLUNTEERS TODAY, all kinds of people are offering their services. The emerging profession of volunteer administration is drawing them into a paid career from a variety of disciplines; anthropology, clergy, psychology, social work, education, recreation, and rehabilitation. Unfortunately, not all community groups nor all paid staff or helping professions are ready for the changes that have overtaken the human services. Volunteers need help to remain with an agency long enough to become really effective advocates for the cause. Without this support when they drop out they can undo the finest public relations efforts. Ironically, with appropriate support volunteers become the best public relations device a cause can have.

With global trends toward decentralization, fragmentation and emphasis on human differences instead of commonalities, human service organizations have been forced to change. At the same time newly formed agencies find developing a sense of community, agreement on issues, and problem solving or decision making a process for which they are ill prepared. Instead of having things done for them, or precise roadmaps or cookbooks, they are having to cope on their own. Money is short and getting shorter, but demands for services are great and growing greater. Beginning in 1972, under revenue sharing, over 37,000 local general purpose government units had money handed to them which they have used in strange and wonderful ways. Only recently have they been receiving assistance and training on how to involve the people in setting priorities. Volunteers who know the community needs from first hand experience or observation have usually been absent from this process. Consequently, ninety-seven per cent of the monies allocated went for things other than people oriented services. "People needs" are very hard to express in cost benefit terms to economists who dominate our modern public policy decision making. Our democracy is being severely tested by the quality of the decisions made at localities, in turn reflected up the line in government and executive offices. Decisions are being made by individuals who do not understand people different from themselves or what could be done for the victims of disability or disaster in prevention and rehabilitation which will be less costly than neglect.

Volunteering is one of the most effective learning methods in the world, a fact to which educators are now giving formal cognizance. Even more important, it is a natural human urge which should be fostered as one of the last areas of life in which compassion and concern for others can be expressed in action. It is a basic human right to be guarded and supported, when necessary, with enabling funding, but not with payment for service, which changes the relationship of the donor to the donee and to the recipient of the service. The essence of volunteering is freedom of choice for the volunteers and for all the other people with whom they might choose to work. Matching the current natural needs of volunteers to the current needs of recipients is an important component in matching resources to needs, and requires a great deal of skill and wisdom.

This book is a series of appeals for order, not chaotic development of the volunteer potential, with strong administrative support. Volunteers cost an initial investment which pays high dividends for everyone involved. A volunteer system must be flexible enough to accommodate all sorts of people in all sorts of settings, stimulating growth and deepening commitment without stifling spontaneity and responsiveness. These factors based on idealism are strong motivating forces that need constant nurturing. Progression for the volunteer means increased trust in and by staff, uncomplicated by salary or economic competition: not displacing staff, but proving out new services and abilities which create new jobs and services.

One meets the nicest people in the world in this kind of occupation and I hope these thoughts express a lifetime of enjoyment from knowing so many of them.

HARRIET H. NAYLOR

1

Volunteerism

A subject dear to my heart is also very important to you and we have some important thinking to do together about volunteers, and how staff can work with volunteers to make the best possible use of their talents and time. Volunteers can make a significant difference in the various agency programs represented here today.

First, I would like to throw out a new word and ask you to incorporate it in your vocabulary. Mr. Webster recognizes the word "voluntarism". A kind of corporate word, it means persons organized together to work toward goals which a group shares. I think that the new word I would like you to consider is "volunteerism" with two "ee's" in it. This, in contrast to "voluntarism", is concerned with the experience of the individual person active in voluntarism in a leadership role, in an administrative role or possibly in direct services to the clients or in supportive services to make programs possible.

We don't speak of volunteer programs but of volunteer services in the agency program, unpaid man-power in the program of the total corporate body. There is unique value added by every individual who serves as a volunteer as well as a staff member. Just as voluntarism is essential for our social fabric and our democratic way of life, I believe that volunteerism is essential for the wholeness of the individual person, and that all persons should have opportunity to give of themselves on behalf of their fellowman no matter what their age or capacity. I am sure there are very few human beings who could not be effective volunteers in some appropriate function. Volunteerism must identify the best function for each

Presented at The Workshop On Volunteer Staff Relations February 25, 1969 individual at his stage of understanding and development. It is this process of identifying and providing the proper function for each individual which I would like to consider as administration of volunteer services, a profession with a basic body of knowledge I call "volunteerism".

Growing Importance of the Direct Service Volunteer

This morning we are not going to concern ourselves about what volunteers do, because volunteers are doing every conceivable kind of task in one agency or another. There are administrative volunteers who serve on boards and committees. There are service volunteers who work in offices. We even have some in state schools for retarded persons repairing bicycles in a bicycle shop. Whatever the skill the volunteer has, I am sure there is some agency, somewhere, which can use it effectively and give him the feeling that he is contributing to a very important program. The volunteers, however, that I would really like to consider most intensively this morning are those who are in direct contact with our clients, whoever they may be and who are giving their service under the auspices of an agency which has a service to offer the whole community. The volunteer has to find an appropriate spot within the total service where he can do well and know that what he is doing is important and valuable to the people he serves.

We have a plurality of volunteers today which is very exciting and opening new vistas for volunteer services epitomized by the federal VISTA program, "Volunteers In Service To America". The new ideas and tremendous capacity for service must be channeled into areas where they can be used appropriately, and volunteers can enjoy their work. If volunteering is not satisfying, there is something wrong. Some new volunteers who have not had a long history of being volunteers have less unlearning to do, with the social revolution we are having today, than some old hands at volunteering.

There is one generality true of all kinds of volunteers today and that is that they are much more interested in action. Volunteers are doers rather than donors, in contrast to traditional patterns in which we always had a few people around who supported our programs with heavy financial contributions but did not really do much else. Support for our programs is less personalized today.

Volunteer skills and aptitudes have a tremendous value through-out our programs, and we don't choose volunteers on the basis of their ability to support financially, but on the basis of their interest, abilities, and concern. We involve people actively in de-termining our service goals so that they will make service goals their own personal objectives, understand how their volunteer work is important, and stay with it. There is nothing more important to the retention of volunteers than their understanding that what volun-teers can do affects the achievement of the agency's objectives.

Volunteers want to learn, want to do a good job, want to fit into the whole. They want to make creative contributions from their own standpoint to the thinking of everyone. They help shape the design for the program as they gain experience. What they think is taken seriously, goes into the hopper and influences the final plans of the agency.

Avoiding Sources of Conflict between Staff and Volunteer

None of us would be here today if we did not see volunteers as essential to our total manpower. It seems to me that my task this morning, then, is to be kind of brutal in pointing up some of the possible points of stress when staff and volunteers try to work to-gether so we can avoid or correct them. I think that we need to face frankly some of the basic assumptions that create misunder-standing. We need to put at rest some of the myths about volunteers so that we can have more real relationships, not masked by myths, no misunderstandings and polite rituals which prevent real com-munication. For this reason, we must recognize some of the differences of perception between the people who are on the payroll of our agencies and those who are not.

The first point of potential stress is the idea of prerogatives. The moment I hear staff or volunteers talking about "their" responsibility or "our" right, I realize that there has been some threat to the individuals involved so that they have become possessive of their functions rather than working in collaborative patterns toward shared goals. They need to be liberated for work together so that they don't worry too much about whose right it is to do what. With our eyes lifted to ultimate goals, we can work together in a flexible and creative way, encouraging each other's participation to accomplish our tasks. Identifying the common interest in agency purpose is a first step.

Another possible stress lies in the threat which volunteers sometimes represent to staff when they are competent and can do the work, and seem to resist control by the staff. Staff is concerned that they will take the ball and run away with it. Staff tends to feel that volunteers may be irresponsible. We constantly hear this word about volunteers. On the other hand volunteers may feel that some of the procedures or policies which they encounter don't make sense, and see the staff wedded to patterns of work which prevent creativity and are too rigid. I think this is particularly likely in casework agencies where the added mystique to the case worker-client relationship awes many volunteers, who then subside into spectator roles instead of active roles in casework services. Only recently are we beginning to involve volunteers with clients in casework agencies. For a long time they simply raised funds or carried on activities related to public relations or program interpretation to the public at large without having any contact with program activities. But, this is changing. Now we are finding that volunteers can be very helpful in service tasks with clients. There is a special contribution volunteers can make because they have freedom to act and time to give and a person-to-person interest in our clients, where they live, might work or have to go for needed services.

Another stress occurs when the staff is perceived as being so expert and so busy that volunteers don't dare ask for help. They feel that staff is inaccessible and does not give enough help for them to do their jobs. They are not told what resources are available and would like more training and help from staff. On the other hand, staff tends to worry about taking on new volunteers because they think the volunteers will need so much time to be helped that they will just add to the demands on staff instead of easing the situation. I think it is possible for staff to spend time with volunteers at the beginning of the volunteer's service and in regularly scheduled contact so that the time required by the volunteer pays off many times over. Volunteer activities relieve staff of tasks and trips, free staff to do those things which only staff can do. And even more important, the service gets an added "human-to-human touch" which makes it more effective.

We have some situations in which volunteers are "used", with the negative connotation that the volunteers are exploited. On the other hand, there is a balance to be maintained between "use" and the other extreme: over-protection and under-placement of volunteers. Often we do not expect enough of volunteers, do not give them enough responsibility, don't delegate authority when we delegate responsibility. Then, they feel demeaned and underestimated by being given a stupid task. So why bother?

Another cause of stress is the feeling on the part of staff that volunteers may get over-involved with a client and his concerns and become advocates of the client against the staff's professional decisions in a kind of anti-establishment role which can be destructive. Some volunteers feel that the professionalism of the staff means they forget that the clients are people with needs which ought to be recognized. Again, these points of conflict are not true in most agencies but the fact that the possibility for them exists gives us some imperative in our administration of volunteer programs to prevent the poor communication which can grow up on such misunderstandings.

Creating a Positive Climate for Volunteers

In a good volunteer setting, volunteers feel that they get more than they give and they seek a chance to grow and to assume important responsibilities. They do not reach this stage unless they have good working relationships with the staff with whom they work. Individualized, in an accepting climate in which to work, they are not pushed too fast, but challenged enough, and given real responsibility and real appreciation for what they can do. Very important in examining problems in communication, and stress between volunteer and staff is the fact that it often boils down to problems in communicating, and the fact that persons behave on the basis of what they believe, rather than facts they may know. Our beliefs are sometimes not even expressed but they are stereotyped assumptions which determine our behavior.

One of the assumptions that ought to be examined is that all volunteers are irresponsible. The phenomenon of "self-fulfilling prophecy" means that people tend to act toward us the way we expect them to act. If we expect volunteers to be irresponsible they are likely to be irresponsible. People are honored and stimulated by high expectations and make a real effort to live up to them.

Another assumption which I think we need to look at is that the volunteers are happy where they are over long periods of time. We don't review volunteer jobs often enough, we don't check out feelings, we don't give people an opportunity to move about and have a variety of experiences. If one is doing a good job we tend to give our attention to someone else. Each volunteer deserves a chance to progress, to grow in responsibilities when his competence grows. Mobility and promotion are most meaningful forms of recognition.

Importance of Supervision and Continuing Training

Service volunteers, to be effective, must be supervised by staff. Staff keep them informed about developments and steer them where they're needed. There must be the same mutual trust and respect to determine the service values which we establish staff to staff. A clue to this kind of mutual respect is the placement of the volunteers, matching abilities to assignments so that people are in the most appropriate position to use their talents and skills and available time most effectively. The appreciation which the staff and the other volunteers have of one volunteer's contribution is a remotivating force which sometimes must be made explicit as well as implicit in trusting the volunteer with further responsibility. We have to guard against pushing volunteers into greater responsibilities before they are ready. Volunteer failure is a very painful and bad experience which does not end with our loss of the volunteer. Often embittered, his version of the experience becomes a negative interpretation of our program in the community. We want to be sure that changes and progression to greater responsibilities are freely accepted, as truly voluntary as initial placement.

An element which contributes to good collaborative relationships is an attitude of openness to learning in all persons. Volunteer or staff, we need opportunities to learn as relevant information is available. Some new roles for volunteers require new forms of learning, not just a classroom setting. Some adults find classrooms uncomfortable because of their past experience. We have discovered that we don't have such a thing as a "fully trained" worker, whether the worker is volunteer or staff. Too much happens too fast these days for anyone to stop learning. What we need is workers open to new developments and new ideas, willing to experiment, flexible about program, policies, and developments, and excited and enthusiastic about innovations in every part of an organization. It is equally important for a Board of Directors to accept the fact that an agency is a "becoming" organization not a finished, polished, inflexible, crystalized organization. Volunteers can contribute from their perspective and insights to new developments and new forms of services important to the goals of the agency.

One device for learning with new volunteers is eliminating the classroom kind of orientation experience until the volunteer expresses a need for more learning. Plunged into apprenticeship roles very quickly, actually on the job under the supervision of more experienced volunteers or staff, volunteers become aware of what their learning needs are before they join groups to learn with other people who have the same learning needs. A block to learning for volunteers is a kind of mystique around what the professional roles are. Volunteers want to participate and they can become extremely adept at reinforcing and strengthening and extending the professional roles as they understand them. A volunteer who has worked with a skilled professional is the best advocate of the need for professional staff. The respect and appreciation developed in harness with good professionals is persuasive in interpreting the need for adequate salary provisions and good personnel policies for staff.

Learning opportunities for staff and volunteers can frequently be shared as a new program emphasis is being developed by an agency. When staff and volunteers learn together about new priorities and implementation of new forms of service, we shake down in our complementary roles together. This kind of experience helps to develop the kinds of respect and mutual trust which have proved so important to collaborative relationships.

Essential to learning for volunteers is the kind of supervision they get in their work. Particularly important for the social work community is the difference from professional supervision. Ways of work in the field of casework, particularly, are not appropriate for supervising volunteers. It is not necessary to develop the professional self-consciousness in volunteers which the professional social worker seeks in professional supervisory relationships. One very wise

psychiatrist remarked that he thought there was certain basic information volunteers had to have to work in a particular setting,
but he pleaded that we not stultify creativity. He didn't want us to
train the spontaneity and common sense out of volunteers because
this was their particular unique value in the program. He did not
want them to be second-rate professionals, but to keep their
identity and perspective as volunteers.

Volunteers who stay with us are those who understand our ground
rules and what we are trying to do. They want to participate in
work toward our goals because they have internalized our goals.
An important personal objective to them is understanding the goals
we share. The kind of supervision that volunteers need must be the
old-fashioned kind which social workers used to speak of as enabling.
The expectations of the volunteer are made realistic, not freezing
or frustrating about his work. We must expect to challenge, stimulate, and encourage the initiative in volunteers. A gradual induction
process increases responsibility as they demonstrate readiness for it.
If we give them too little responsibility they will be bored and feel
demeaned by the process. If we give them too much, they will be
overwhelmed. Again, the professional skill involved is a balance
between two extremes.

Avoiding assumptions which determine our behavior without our
being aware of them, in our work together we can control and very
consciously develop explicit descriptions of our mutual responsibilities. Defining congruency, contiguity, and the outer limits of each set
of responsibilities makes staff clear about what is expected of
them and volunteers clear about what is expected of them. Both
understand when they are supposed to be working together and when
they are working independently. These areas may shift so we have to
review and revise and renew these definitions periodically and be
aware of the need to shift as volunteers grow in capacity. Program
emphases may shift, too. Realistic expectations by each person of
the work of the other will facilitate their collaboration.

It is essential for free communication between staff and volunteers
to schedule regular opportunities for individual consultations, for
mutual discussion, testing of ideas, redirection of efforts and adjustment of work loads. We are moving toward group supervision of
volunteers because the group experience develops a sense of identity

among the volunteers. The thinking of the whole group is valuable to all of the members in proportion to the degree each is given a chance to air concerns, share insights and solutions to problems. We remember best what we say at a meeting, not what we heard someone else say.

Another scheduled process should be an automatic review of the work being done, focussed not on the person in the job, but the work. Implications for the person in the job are there but it is much easier to readjust the work than to readjust the person. In the beginning, we worked with the person to develop common expectations which now can be used as a yardstick to measure accomplishments in a periodic work review. The work review may result in promotional opportunity for the volunteer, a regrouping of the tasks, cutting back some of the responsibility, or restating some of the objectives with new emphases as the needs are shifting and changing over a period of time. Review gives us the basis for real recognition of each person for his unique individual contributions, given through both tangible and intangible means.

Decentralized Administration of Volunteers

As volunteer services grow, our administration may need decentralization. This means that the staff member responsible for volunteers will continue in the recruitment and orientation and in the development of volunteer opportunities for the volunteers. However, on-the-job supervision of the volunteer and the help which the volunteer may need as he carries this job, must be given by the people in charge of the area to which the volunteer has been assigned. The orientation becomes much more general, a ground rules approach to the field of service which the agency is engaged in, to the agency and its history and its ways of work and general policies. These may change from time to time and we may have to bring volunteers back for reorientation as new services and policies are evolved. The actual job training, then, happens in the work area and is given as the need arises, sometimes individually and sometimes in groups.

Essential for the staff in the work area is skill delegation, so that people are inducted into their responsibilities comfortably, experience success from effectiveness, and get some feedback about their worth early in their experience. They need satisfaction to grow and to build their capacity to carry greater responsibility. As time goes on this induction process will mean that the volunteer worker will need less and less close supervision. There will be a collaborative relationship with the people in the work area which can be very mutually satisfying.

The work review involves the supervisor in the work area, the volunteer and a report back to the Coordinator of Volunteers, stating whether this placement is to continue, the nature of any changes which have been decided on and the readjustment of the assignment if necessary. Overall recognition plans should be carried by the Coordinator and not decentralized. One of the best recognition plans I have heard about recently is the one in which the volunteers gave a recognition party to the staff who had helped them to enjoy their volunteer work so much.

Broader Participation by Volunteers

You see, it is possible to get over some of the communication blocks and to develop patterns of work together which contribute to accomplishment of the agency's purposes and development and full self-actualization of the volunteers themselves. I think we are giving more and more recognition to volunteers who give service in direct relationships rather than to board members who used to get all of the glory.

We are realizing the significance of volunteering as an expression of idealism in the volunteer. The vision which the volunteers have of how things ought to be is a measure for our services. We ought to tap this perspective as we evaluate our total services. Every day the newspapers feature the negative aspects of human nature. We don't read enough about the other side of human nature, in which volunteerism discloses human beings at their best, which makes working with volunteers such a satisfying job. I am very much concerned that we do not abjectly accept what newspapers say about people not wanting to be involved. They do, they just don't know how.

I would like to read to you from a book called "Reclaiming The American Dream" by Richard C. Cornuelle who develops the theory that the part of human nature which is motivated by ideals and concern for our fellow humans is not recognized in our social planning. He comments,

"The service motive seems weak only because we have failed to find ways to apply it to complex modern problems. We see it at work only in simple 19th Century ways and this contributes to the illusion that the independent sector is unfit for modern responsibility."

"New vision in developing personal outlets for the service is desperately needed. Their decline sharply constricts the scope of the human enterprize, a man who only works and votes and pays his taxes is scarcely a whole man. 'Reverence for life', says Dr. Schweitzer, in his persistent way, 'demands from all that they should sacrifice a portion of their own life for others.' But now, increasingly, we can only help our fellowmen through middle-men, through remote political institutions. Lacking a direct outlet for our hunger to help others, to add the full dimension of meaning to our lives, we are frustrated and incomplete. . . .

. . . The demand of the future is to release the idealistic willpower, as Schweitzer called it, which has been bottled up with such alarming human consequences. We need first of all to identify the force which can give direction to the untapped power of the service motive."

It is my firm belief that each of us here today represents an agency whose goals can be the force needed to give direction to the untapped power of the service motive. Thousands of persons need an opportunity to become volunteers, need to be givers as well as receivers in our world today, need some way of relating to their fellowman. Knowing that what they do makes a difference to persons and that it is important how they serve. If the agencies' services can be offered, they can play an essential part.

Each of us today has a responsibility to look at our own practices in the administration of the volunteer services in our agency, to be sure that every person who serves with us has a good experience, that he is working consciously toward our agency objectives, and that he has taken those objectives and made them his own. Together we can have the gratification of knowing that we have performed important tasks which supplement one another. The people who are performing those tasks each have a distinctive and unique contribution to make. We have to insure that these contributions are made available for our services.

Channeling Professional and Volunteer Skills Toward Common Goals

As a social worker, I am concerned about the perspective which social work seems to have about volunteers: we take 'em if we have to, but not unless we have to. Tha parallel exists in other fields, and perhaps this example from industry will illustrate our situation.

One of the paper companies is aware that the process of making paper pollutes streams and the atmosphere around a paper mill. However, the company has a policy that it will conform with the laws and regulations as they are developed by the government, but it will not take any initiative about anti-pollution measures. This decision was made a couple of years ago and suddenly that company is waking up to the fact that the laws and regulations which are being passed by public demand are very uncomfortable for the paper industry because they are being made by people who do not understand how to make paper. If the company had been involved in the policy-making regulations, if they had embarked on their own research to find the most effective ways to control pollution, the means of control would be much more palatable to that paper company.

Our parallel in this as social workers involves the attitude of social work toward volunteers. The 1967 Harris amendments to the Social Security Act mandated volunteers in public assistance and child welfare programs which have never used volunteers before. The attitude of some of the people on those staffs is "if we've got to have them we will put up with them, but we will get just as little involved with them as possible".

The volunteers are going to be there and they are going to be concerned with what is going on. We will be much more effective in our total services if we "get with" the volunteers in our planning, thinking together on designs for services. As Mr. Cornuelle says, there is a tremendous power waiting to be tapped. We can either work with it or we can regard it as an outside force which we don't want to be involved with. The fact that it is powerful and it is going to become more powerful as time goes on is a fact of life today.

To me it is the hope of the future that volunteers are becoming more deeply involved throughout our programs. We are all going to benefit from what they can bring. We need this powerful source to solve the overwhelmingly serious and comprehensive social problems which we face today. Therefore, administration of volunteer services becomes the means we have for channeling this power, for directing this effort toward common goals rather than towards goals which will conflict with ours, which have been developed out of significant experience. It is up to us whether we will be with it or a'gin it and I think we had better be and are going to be, with it.

2

VOLUNTARY ACTION FOR THE MENTALLY DISABLED

Popularized volunteering is regarded as a mixed blessing by many professionals in the field of mental health. In hospital and community mental health programs, as volunteering becomes the "in" thing to do, all sorts of people offer help, and most staff are unprepared to use it well. Some staff, misled by myths about volunteers, feel that their professional practice is in danger of being vitiated by lowered standards of dilettante or ignorant laymen. Some feel that their jobs are in jeopardy from highly qualified people who may be seeking to demonstrate competence in order to be hired. Others appreciate the potential value in this additional help and are secure enough to make the best use of the wide range of talent available from private citizens willing to give their time. With enthusiasm, they plan for assignments, orientation and training to give volunteers knowhow and confidence to contribute appropriately. Such initial time investment pays real dividends in volunteer time contributed later which frees the paid staff for technical and diagnostic activities. Most important, practice without volunteers deprives patients of relationships important to their recovery and deprives staff of allies in the community who would go to bat for beleaguered budgets, for essential staff skills.

Opportunities for creative and meaningful service attract volunteers and give them a chance to relate to others in ways they may not enjoy vocationally or in their ordinary life situations. Many a volunteer finds that he really did make enough difference to keep alive the latent rescue fantasy which probably motivates many volunteers in the first place. When a patient makes real progress because of his help, this is the most gratifying form of thanks to a volunteer.

Volunteering is being accelerated nationally by the National Center for Voluntary Action with its network of local Voluntary Action Centers and such legislation as Title I in the Elementary and Secondary Education Act and the Harris amendments to Social Security. Volunteers are making possible many community activities in mental health and retardation services. Competition is growing keener. The ranks of traditional, predictable volunteers are decreasing, while at the same time new kinds of persons are emerging as volunteers, stimulated by the urgency of today's problems. Everybody wants to *do* something. Students want to apply their ideals. Senior citizens do not want to waste their life wisdom after retirement. The disadvantaged want to improve service delivery and make service relevant to the needs they understand so well.

Convinced that mental as well as physical health is a basic human right, concerned citizens want to extend this right to all persons. Some gain support for appropriate services, serve on boards of voluntary associations, organize to interpret. Some work one-to-one in direct service, and some volunteers are doing both. Now distinction is made between service volunteers and policy makers, and between governmental and private services. Consumers and their lay advocates participate in policy development and planning. Service roles are more directly involved with the victims of handicaps, but sometimes are devoted to functions like fund raising, removed from them. Direct firsthand response from patients motivates volunteers and deepens their commitment; they find themselves encouraging people to utilize services and mobilizing the resources of the community to meet their needs.

The N.I.M.H. study, NON-PROFESSIONAL PERSONNEL IN MENTAL HEALTH PROGRAMS, documents the value of volunteers as well as para-professionals to supplement staffing in mental health programs. Its typology of functions reflects new roles: CARE TAKING such as feeding, escorting patients; not only in hospital settings but in the community and at the volunteer's own home.

SOCIAL SUSTENANCE: personal continuing relationships such as friend-to friend or foster grandparent who encourages efforts toward self-help, independence, and competence; PROFES-SIONAL ASSISTANTS serve within a discipline as an extension of professional time and effort by volunteers, such as case aide under case worker, or medical aide. BRIDGING volunteers use and develop community resources and offer developmental experiences outside institutions which give patients courage to enter the main-stream of community life.

In addition to these four functions I see another called ADVOCACY, for volunteers. Concerned citizens accomplish wonders as pleaders for the mentally handicapped because they are perceived by both patients and the public as free from paid job interests, professional status needs, or clinical perspectives. Volunteers can cut through red tape and influence important decisions, of individuals, as a patient considering whether to use a service, and of groups such as a county legislature considering the community mental health center budget. The volunteer advocate speaks more freely than paid staff, as participating citizen and potential consumer.

It takes secure administrators to share with their public their problems as well as their successes. Special events to which the public is invited usually show only the pleasant aspects of facilities and programs, sending potential volunteers home again assured everything is going so well that they are not needed. We could enlist powerful advocates for adequate staffing and for the initiation or continuation of experimental programs, if private citizens under-stood these needs. Volunteers speak to budget makers and legislators about the impact on the mentally handicapped people they know personally from firsthand experience, which gives them authenticity. Comprehensive health planning needs such informed, concerned citizens to speak for the mentally handicapped who cannot speak for themselves.

One block to accepting volunteers is the uneasy idea within professions that the public expects them not to need help—that they ought to be able to do the job alone. The unique value of unpaid staff is not explicit in most academic curricula, nor in many intern or preceptorship experiences. Yet active practitioners face a need for help and it is readily available from potential volunteers in most practice settings. Professional education at every level from basic professional education throughout inservice and continuing education opportunities, in professional association conferences and mixed staff groupings should build realistic expectations about the use of volunteer manpower, as unique, and valuable, rather than a threat to standards, or to jobs!

Training and supervision for volunteers must be tailored to the volunteer perspective, not simply to meet the staff need to tell them what to do! Volunteers face a variety of claims on their time, and a network of obligations in their homes and communities. Through what we professionals teach, they develop interest and concern and an active desire to give their time to our programs. Training must not destroy volunteer spontaneity and common sense but give confidence in self and in readily available help. Progress to more important responsibilities comes as volunteers demonstrate competence and willingness for deeper involvement. Progress can be to administrative roles, such as taking on new volunteers as apprentices, training new staff about working with volunteers or recruiting other volunteers and community support. One of the most coveted volunteer jobs in one system is that of "Floater". Through experience in many different aspects of the program, the Floater becomes qualified as backup staff in several areas so that no person need be disappointed if some volunteer, originally assigned, finds that his primary obligation keeps him from his volunteer job. Volunteers must be deployed more richly than paid staff for such contingencies.

Volunteer imagination and fresh perspectives enrich program development. The volunteer brings a non-technical "human to human" perception with a neutrality invaluable to interdisciplinary teams whose other members each have special clinical or activity perspectives. The volunteer frequently understands the background of the patient, what traditions and history determine the attitudes and quality of his community life. This advocacy interprets to staff the patient in context of community. Cultural values can vary from one block to another within a catchment area. The volunteer who really knows a program can recommend it to neighbors. Volunteers innovate services using their knowledge of available community resources.

Volunteers come into programs not from a vacuum, but from a network of community connections: to family, organizations, church, ethnic group, etc. Thus, one volunteer converted may give a program director access to a great many influential groups in the community. Volunteers with several reference groups organize "adhocracies" to accomplish their goals by persuading fellow members of several groups to work together on a project. Members are urged to recruit volunteers by chapters of the Mental Health Association or the Association For Retarded Citizens. Conversely, service volunteers, aware of needs for concerted action, join community organizations with related objectives and goals. The volunteer member of an association is a two-way link for that association with the service where he volunteers. Casual advocacy among members is influential because it is authenticized by firsthand testimony of the volunteer. Nothing reinforces credibility like knowing the speaker. Voluntary Action Centers taught to understand the needs of the mentally handicapped, are important allies in communities. Service organizations such as JC's. PTA's, Veteran Auxiliaries, have specific interest in mental health and retardation. Their locals recruit for and support services whose goals, accomplishments and potential they understand and believe in.

Volunteering helps most individuals as much as it enriches the services within which they give their time and effort. In volunteering, people discover skills and capacities they hadn't known they had. The right to volunteer, to be on the giving end, should be extended to all, not only a privilege for persons who are already quite advantaged. Varied and appropriate service opportunities are needed for patients, their families, for young people to work with younger people, for people to work together on projects, to discover commonality with others quite different from themselves. Nonprofessional manpower can extend and reinforce the work of professionals and free professionals for practice where their full qualifications are essential. Volunteers benefit the mentally handicapped and also help themselves develop social equilibrium; in this sense, volunteering is primary prevention for volunteers. The delinquent boy feels better about himself by helping patients in a state hospital; the senior citizen slows senescence while his love and skill move retarded children to achieve levels of competence which they probably would not otherwise even attempt.

Mental health parallels health concepts of prevention. At the primary level, volunteering maintains and develops social competence. Secondary prevention maintains and develops strength to reduce crisis or acute illness. Volunteers help patients preserve and enhance self-concepts, retain connections with home and community during residential care, and offer activities to preserve abilities not damaged by the illness. Tertiary prevention, to limit disability and reduce chronicity, is especially dramatic with the long term resident of an institution. Remotivation and habilitation involve simple life skills taught by volunteers to supplement and reinforce staff efforts to develop social awareness and competence. Coping skills of normal living can be taught with little special training, in rehabilitation. Parties, so valuable for the mentally handicapped, wherever possible should be a result of *their* planning with volunteers, rather than unexpected events which may not fit well with the rest of their treatment program.

Most professions have goals for service which could be reached more quickly with help to follow through after the diagnostic and prescriptive process is completed. The volunteer helps people test themselves by responding as a practical, human to human neighbor, not like a clinician with discipline and restraint. Self-perceptive understanding may be the most valuable kind of social sustenance which a volunteer can offer. Teaching living skills, stimulating practice, encouraging forays into unfamiliar settings, helping people develop independent judgment, all are gratifying functions for volunteers. Next steps include developing job openings, finding living arrangements, and giving the ex-patient confidence to join organizations and move into interests of his own.

Good experience with staff partners makes volunteers articulate advocates of standards for trained staff, for program experiments and for projects at budget hearings. Volunteers recruit staff to "their" programs by demonstrating support and interest and to disciplines by enthusiasm for professionals they have known. Volunteers, accustomed to working in committees, have more experience at shared decision-making than many people in professions allied under a medical technocracy.

Their participation as equals, with their unique perspective to contribute, helps keep plans realistic and relevant. One such coordinated effort involves a state hospital, a community clinic, a Mental Health chapter and a YWCA in one community. Patients move from an in-hospital group into a community social group living in a protected residence from which individuals spin off as regular members into interest groups as they resume normal life, all with volunteers and staff helping. Such partnership means dominance by neither volunteer nor staff but mutual respect, trust and liking: a *we,* not *they* tone. Common goals, clear and congruent, make the difference, with free communication horizontal as well as vertical, informal as well as formal. Training of staff and volunteers together builds this kind of teamwork, with periodic review of the staff and complementary volunteer roles and open opportunities for movement and advancement for both.

Where recognition for staff means salary raises and promotions, for volunteers it takes a variety of forms. Seeing patients progress is the most important factor in their staying with a job. To be entrusted with greater responsibility is another. Some volunteers say being counted on by patient and by staff is what keeps them coming. Explicit thanks as well as implicit should be expressed by the top leadership of a program. Parties for volunteer families, letters to employers, and records on services for college applications, employers or teachers recognize volunteer effort. Telling other people whose feelings are significant to the volunteer means a great deal to the volunteer, as well as whatever is done for him directly or tangibly with pins or certificates to acknowledge his special characteristics, abilities, and contributed time.

Good administration of volunteer service centralizes administrative leadership, and decentralizes supervision on the job. To humanize services, volunteers help us as staff to see the patient first as a person, as well as from our own special and different perspective. Volunteers can offer human, spiritual and aesthetic experiences which service budgets can never cover. People with mental handicaps need the creativity and fresh viewpoint of volunteers. Volunteers need a chance to be involved, to be needed, to do important work and to be valued. If we as staff want their input, then we are going to have to be sure that we are the kind of people who give volunteers support, a chance to learn and appropriate recognition. There's great work to be done, together!

Mrs. Harriet H. Naylor as
Director of Volunteer Services
NYSD Mental Hygiene

3

THE VOLUNTEER AS ADVOCATE

The possibilities for strengthening programs by volunteer advocacy are growing out of experience in community action programs and governmental services as well as more traditional voluntary agencies. Acting as advocates or interpreters, volunteers serve clients directly, help people find appropriate services, or mobilize resources in their behalf.

In all the kinds of human services the volunteer serves as advocate for services with people and their families from the earliest prevention level throughout treatment, and continues to help persons to confidence and competence throughout the rehabilitation process. Articulating needs the victim of unfortunate circumstances may not be able to express, interpreting the nature of services and intent of providers of services, the volunteer serves as interpreter in both directions, facilitating the use of services and maximizing their impact.

Volunteer advocates can extend staff outreach efforts. Gate-keepers in communities, those key persons whose approval is essential before a service is accepted by their neighbors, can persuade families to use services which may be new, or offered outside their immediate community. This kind of advocacy helps preventive services to be used early before situations become aggravated or chronic.

Volunteers at the point of intake can often allay the fears of patients and their families. Understanding their feelings when a program is initiated, they can reassure people in a stressful situation when the paid staff is too busy. An ex-client is particularly valuable in this assignment since firsthand experience as a consumer gives his testimonial authenticity. Later on, a volunteer can maintain motivation for use of services as a friend without clinical or job objectives, perceived by the current consumer as therefore more credible.

Volunteers don't come to us from a vacuum. The network of connections most volunteers have provides opportunities for telling their relatives, neighbors and fellow members the values and gratifications in being a volunteer. As advocates, volunteers persuasively recruit people as both staff and as other volunteers for their cause. Such interpretation of the service may be public education for their service club, church fellow members or a coffee klatch. But coming from someone already known and accepted, with firsthand experience and observations, the message is much more likely to be accepted.

Volunteer advocates, too, may present the culture and tradition of a community to staff who may not have roots there or know what has gone on there before. Sometimes cultural patterns determine attitudes toward a service which may block effective use of that service. Staff may jump to the conclusion that parents are not interested in their children, when they do not follow their progress by visits and seeking consultation. A volunteer can explain how difficult it is there to get transportation, or pay for it, or to come at times when staff is available for consultation. Many times hours could be adjusted to the cultural patterns of an area. There are values and attitudes unique to communities which paid staff must understand to communicate effectively.

Perhaps the most telling volunteer advocacy comes at the social action level. Defined as "class advocacy", volunteer activities can impact community priorities and mobilize constituencies in support of special needs. This may mean expressing needs of persons in such a way as to persuade service professionals to make themselves available and tailor their service to those needs. This may mean persuading budget makers and decision makers at local, state, and even national legislative levels that services are needed and deserve budgetary support.

We on staff have a tendency to present our best side when we are interpreting our services to the public. If we really want to enlist volunteers as advocates, it is essential that we also share our problems and our aspirations with citizens so that they understand what our needs and frustrations are, as well as our tangible accomplishments. Through our risking such trust in volunteers, they take on our staff goals and objectives when they have a voice in formulating them. Work by volunteers can be more direct in ways closed to paid staff. Volunteers frequently cut through protocol, red tape, the limitations of position on a structure chart, right to the people who can effect real change in a community, or who control support for the provision of services.

The volunteer represents a source of strength in gaining public support for services, in insuring that services are designed realistically and relevantly for needs, and persuading the target group to use those services. Training for staff in enlisting volunteer advocacy is crucial to enjoying this fringe benefit of volunteer services.

4

Voluntary Action Centers

Last night Mrs. Dills of San Francisco told a very interesting experience she had had on the elevator, about the VOLUNTEER ATLANTA button she was wearing. Somebody, not one of us obviously, asked her what VOLUNTEER was and she was somewhat taken aback because we all think we all know what a volunteer is. She said, "This is someone who works and gives service without pay." The man simply beamed at her, and said, "I think that's the sweetest think I've ever heard." Now maybe this is a fresh viewpoint on volunteering, but I have a hunch that a sign my husband used to have on his office wall applies here: "The Major Problem In Communication Is The Illusion That It Has Already Been Achieved." We think people know about volunteers and we think they know about our problems, and they don't.

There isn't any cookbook for a Voluntary Action Center and there isn't any map to show you how to get there. In your packets are general guidelines, to describe how you may start in your own area. We're going to mix you up thoroughly to discuss in groups. I would like to start you thinking a little bit about what the implications are in new trends in the field of volunteers and what they mean to those of us who have been associated with volunteer bureaus and those of us who have not. VACs are really going to involve citizens in designing their own destiny by meaningful relationships with

*For three days in Atlanta in September, 1970, some 150 leaders from 30 U.S. cities convened for the First Community Workshop on Voluntary Action Centers. This event, sponsored by the National Center for Voluntary Action, bids to be a landmark in the annals of American voluntarism.

The general purpose of the Workshop was to explore the concept and feasibility of local Voluntary Action Centers—centralized bodies that would serve as the prime link between a community's volunteer reserve and all of its agencies with jobs to do—and as a focal point for maximizing the total contributions of its volunteer resources.

fellow citizens in developing services that are relevant for today's needs and not yesterday's. There are an awful lot of agencies today preoccupied with their own survival and with meeting un-needs because they know how. It seems to me that the volunteer at every level in the scene today who says that because we do have agencies that are not listening, the days of voluntarism are over. Voluntarism is dead, long live volunteerism is the new trend: new kinds of volunteers to do new kinds of services. I think of voluntarism with an "a" as a corporate concept and with the "ee" as related to the individual volunteer. Just as our democratic pluralistic society needs voluntarism so people need volunteerism as a part of their life experience.

We have a vast reservoir of know-how about volunteers residing in the Volunteer Bureaus. They've led in this field, I think, because all of them have been doing some of the things that we are now feeling are appropriate for VAC's to do: But there is a principle of geographic justice: what if you live in a place where there isn't a Volunteer Bureau, or a place where there aren't services that you can volunteer for readily? Let's see how we can bring people together to plan, to set objectives, and to find a slot in which each can make a contribution. But let's not ignore the wisdom from years of experience in Volunteer Bureaus where the principle of volunteer-staff partnership and voluntary-governmental partnership has been applied for a long time, with ways of sharing leadership as described in "Future Shock" as "adhocracy": I assume the leadership when it's my skills and my knowledge and my perceptions that are going to be most helpful. Somebody connects me with the people who will be carrying out programs, so that what I put in can be perceived in the program as it is developed.

Another kind of knowledge that the Volunteer Bureaus have developed to a high degree is the process of developing volunteers and of valuing mobility of volunteers from one service to another, not a career ladder in sequential steps in one agency, but in a lattice of horizontal mobility as well as vertical. The bureau itself has a beautifully neutral spot in a community in that it is non-medical, non-social work, and its focus is on people rather than organizations. The major contributions that the volunteer bureaus have made to our society is that they have given a lot of people real experience with volunteers, exploding myths about volunteers and unfair assumptions that are made about them. They have really taught through living experience, faith and trust in volunteers. There aren't enough volunteer bureaus.

There is something going for us in this field, in the popularity of volunteering today, that I think we can tap, but there is also a real ambivalence about it. We might as well face ambiguity squarely. In the first place, we have not seen a way to bring people together in assessing voluntarism from the *volunteer's* standpoint. A lot of volunteers would like to know, "What difference did it make that I served, how are my objectives becoming part of the objectives of services in the community, who listens to me in the planning process?" This is one of the new imperatives. Another evidence of ambivalence is that we have a good many legal bases for volunteers in programs, but we haven't had the implementing appropriations made. This is true in dramatic form in the new RSVP program in Title VI of the Older Americans Act. There is a plan there which came about because some senior citizen volunteers felt that their experience was so valuable to them as persons that they went and testified in Congressional hearings. RSVP landed on the books under Title VI as the Reid Amendments, but the enabling appropriations have not been forthcoming. I would challenge all of us: are we going to wait for that? Are we going to let older persons slip into senescence because they are not aware how badly they are needed? Or are we going to do something about it locally? In the welfare field, the Harris Amendments to the Social Security Act were passed in 1967, but as of January 1, only seventeen states had volunteers in operations. There has been a tremendous growth of volunteers in the courts, which have come full circle in the concept of probation because the original probation people were volunteers: and then professionals assumed full responsibility: from 27 courts about four years ago, now over 2,000 have volunteers. But those persons who are giving leadership to this movement are beginning to say we need a guild for volunteers, a channel for volunteers to express their convictions about human needs to make a real difference. Perhaps the only way they can do it is through their own organization, not through any existing one. More ambivalance exists in three national organizations interested in volunteers and the development of a profession for volunteer administration. They're having some of the same territorial rights problems that the professions are having now on inter-disciplinary teams. The American Association of Volunteer Service Coordinators, spawned by the American Psychiatric Association, met last week in Philadelphia. There was real anguish about a very simple modification of the membership regulations in that organization, to broaden them to include persons administering volunteer programs for the physically handicapped as well as in mental health and retardation. A loose category of associate membership is not allowed to vote or to change the direction of the organization. Almost the same thing happened in the parallel organization, for general hospitals, The Society for Directors of Volunteer Services, spawned by the American Hospital Association. They, too, have an associate membership. The issue facing us now is whether we are going to have an umbrella organization of some sort, whether we are going to live the principle we believe of partnership at all levels or whether we are going to have a number of small groups of people who are confusing the field in which they practice with the nature of a profession. The VACs are going to be able to give us some real insights about what is required of this new profession, and I hope they will take the lead in developing learning opportunities for people who practice it.

We speak of partnership, but we have some very fuzzy lines between public and private services. In my own field of mental health, we have public agencies offering services, and we have voluntary agencies offering services on a fee basis or with grants from government tax funds on which they are absolutely dependent. We have in the medical field a real cleavage between auxiliary volunteers (who don't think of themselves as volunteers at all) and service volunteers.

We have a consumer revolution in our land, and I think many of these possessive and ingrown perspectives are going to be shaken up because people who are beneficiaries of services or *not* beneficiaries of services are no longer willing to remain unserved, poorly served or disadvantaged. Some of us are wary of the "cost-benefit" approach in the traditional agencies, but there are people around who are asking a very legitimate question: "What are we getting for all that money?" Who is being served? It seems to me our part of this is an ethical question for all of us to do some soul-searching about: How many times we are applying volunteers as band-aids when major surgery is indicated? Volunteers who are serving in palliative roles come to identify very closely with the people who are not being well served. But we have not yet provided an avenue for them to express this concern. It seems to me that the VAC in a community is the agency to take this leadership.

The trend today is for comprehensive planning, particularly in the health and rehabilitation fields. Who are the laymen who are mandated on those planning groups? What responsibility are we taking to be sure that the consumer viewpoint is there, and not in name only? I could name you one board that has a lot of doctors' wives on the board to represent the consumer in a medical service. I just don't think that's fair.

Once we have the concept that in-service volunteers have a special perspective that we need in planning, staffs get worried. They begin to worry about volunteers as watchdogs or spies. They need to develop their own leadership skills so that the volunteers who are there take on staff goals and become advocates for the whole service, for people, and not adversaries to staff but allies. And I have enough faith in good intentions of people to think that staff goals are valid. It's the way they're working toward them that misses fire sometimes, and advocates would help more than adversaries. Teamwork.

Another symptom of society's ambivalence is the push for advocacy in social action, while limiting by new tax laws the activities of any agency dependent on a foundation. The section that is becoming the bugaboo of many foundations, 501 C3, says that a foundation becomes subject to tax for efforts to influence legislation through attempts to affect the opinion of the general public. How are we going to get around this one? I don't have answers. I told you there was no cookbook! But this is a very real problem in many communities.

Let's look at advocacy of volunteers a little bit, because it is essential at every level. In the first place, the volunteer as ombudsman can help a person use a service. Let him know what services are available and that they're meant for him, not somebody else.

The volunteer, knowing the community, knowing what's gone on there before, can say to the professionals and services, "This is what this community requires, this is what happened here before. We've tried that, or haven't really thought that one through here." It's up to the skill of the pros then to say why they really offer something valid and new that will work when something didn't work there before.

Another advocacy role of the volunteer is help in problem *solving*— and the accent is on the second word—in a rational approach, but not just in identifying problems. Our habit in community planning has been to put names and labels on problems and to then consider them solved. The VACs are going to help move people into the action stage of solutions and not get stuck testing alternatives and never getting into the action phase.

We have had very presumptive methods of recruiting and placing volunteers for many years. You'll find them in my own writings; people are constantly chiding me! Marshall McLuhan says the printed page is the rear view mirror. How I wish I could call that book back and put some other things in it!—for I talked there about identifying appropriate *tasks* for volunteers. I think we've outgrown task assignments. If we haven't, the volunteer very quickly outgrows us because it is very presumptive to limit him in this way. I think we have to trust the outcome if we assign volunteers to a total function within their range of choice, and quickly help them develop leadership influence from their volunteer experience. We used to have what I called the Whew! method of placing volunteers. (You know, you got a piano player for Friday night and you said "Whew" and you forgot him!) In my survey of the state hospitals in New York State when I went on my job I found one woman who had been doing that for 17 years. I don't think this should happen to anybody. It's true, she might have chosen again and again that piano-playing assignment, but when I asked her if anybody had ever asked her if she wanted to do anything different, she said, "No, because they don't have to worry about Friday nights." This is true, they didn't.

Another element on the scene today is our looking at what is meaningful recognition. We have a lot of certificates, we have a lot of pins and Sunday School bars, but volunteers are telling us loud and clear that it really means something to them to be trusted with real responsibility, not protected from it; to be given new volunteers to orient to a program; to be given people to teach, especially the staff; to be given responsibility at a budget meeting for representing in an advocacy role the people being served in a program the volunteer is in. So, one of our responsibilities in the VACs is going to be to help people in a transition of their perspective from themselves in just one job, doing a particular task, to seeing themselves as essential for change in that community. The skills that this is going to require have got to be developed outside of their own organization as well as in. Opportunity for the volunteer to see beyond the job he's on impels him to take up the cudgels when necessary on behalf of the people whose needs he knows at first hand.

Volunteers need access to program planning. Many innovative programs have developed because of their perspectives. I'm thinking of a beautiful one that's just coming up now in the field of retardation. It is not easy to live with a retarded child. It is not easy to give a retarded child up to an institution. Volunteers have perceived that you can make it if you have a little time off from time to time. So springing up across the country are respite homes. Sometimes this function rotates among parents of retarded children and sometimes they have established an agency. But it was their perception of the very human need of a family for relief from an overburdening problem, and their perception of a need to preserve that family that developed a new service which has many implications for other services: Why do we separate older couples and institutionalize older persons? What kinds of services can volunteers conceive to keep older couples taking care of one another with a little help from their friends, the volunteers?

One of the things that is a real challenge to us (and all of you in this room have this kind of responsibility because you are all in leadership roles) is to give volunteers a better self-image, a feeling about themselves so that they'll have the confidence to speak up, so that they will know that what they know as truth from first-hand experience, is also important to other persons. We've got to find a way to give people some access to administrators of programs at every level, some means of communicating their observations. We've reached a point today at which we can say that volunteering is no longer a privilege of the already privileged, but a basic human right.

This has implications for how we operate a VAC, because we are not screening people out but counseling them in, matching needs with their ability to do something about those needs. We can see what it does for older persons. One little old lady volunteer said to me, "I climbed right off the shelf to be a volunteer!" Delinquent boys in a state training school are volunteers on a one-to-one basis with regressed patients in a State Hospital. The way those boys feel about themselves, once they have found that they are needed and that they have much to give, is important for *all* persons.

Stereotypes still haunt us. They lead us into failing to test our assumptions about sex roles. What do we let men do as volunteers, and women? We put a ceiling on people that they don't need, especially the aged and the young. I hear people talking about how they are so careful to screen out the dirty hippies from hospitals. And yet, I could show you one of the most immaculate, starched nurses you ever did see who was simply desperate the day some college kids turned up as volunteers. She says, "If I hadn't been so desperate I never would have let it happen." But she now would tell you that, " . . . those kids are still here, some of them every day of the week. They are so concerned because they feel that what a society does for the least of its members is the test of that society, and that the severely retarded people in a state school are that least."

We took a bus load of Aid to Families with Dependent Children mothers to a state hospital. They had all asked for transportation money to go because they had someone they wanted to visit there—a relative of their own or a neighbor's child. So we said OK, we'll get a bus, but you'll have to visit a patient who hasn't been visited in a long time as well as the one you're going to see. It was a 50-mile bus trip, and while they rode, some very careful assignments were made. Out of that, we had several patients who have reestablished their ties back in Brooklyn, but even more beautiful was the mother who said to me when she walked back to the bus after visiting, "It's been a long time since I thought I had anything to give anybody and I'm coming back next time just to see my *patient*." When we called these people together with a couple of "experts" to ask questions, the first five questions were related to "is it OK to give those patients money?" This from people who are on welfare or who had taken a day off from work without pay in order to go!

Our untested assumption had been that we shouldn't ask them to volunteer, and how wrong it had been!

There's another assumption rampant now, that all of us are going to have to test. With budgets tightening up, we must protect the voluntary sector: people are assuming they are going to save money with volunteers. And we do have a job to do there because volunteers don't save money *except* as they improve services and make them more effective. It takes some money to have a volunteer program, to make it possible for all persons to volunteer even if they need out-of-pocket expenses, transportation, or baby sitting. But on the other hand, budget cuts are going to mean that some services will be entrusted to volunteers which wouldn't have been assigned under other circumstances. We will have some breakthroughs in what new jobs volunteers can do, so it may not be an entirely negative picture when agencies are being pressed financially.

Ideas are changing to a concept of *human* services, rather than fragmenting people with health services, education services, child welfare services, etc. There is a major shift from thinking of services as directed to acute needs, to a new focus on prevention and rehabilitation. The National Institutes of Health have defined prevention in a way that is dear to my heart: It's to the effect that prevention is the maintenance of health. Secondary prevention is the meeting of acute need, and the prevention of chronicity. Tertiary prevention is the prevention of deterioration, the kind of paralysis and ossification that happens to people when they've had a problem for a long time. Volunteers are needed all along the way. Rehabilitation cannot take place without human relationships.

I don't know how many of you are aware of what's been happening in Great Britain's child welfare services, but they are about to be totally reorganized. Every locality is going to be held responsible for giving all services to all persons from 0 to 18 years of age. No buck-passing up to the state. (Of course, they don't have a state level, but up to the National Government.) Problems must be solved in the locality. Crucial to this plan and its effectiveness are the Citizens Advisory Bureaus in Great Britain which are 99% volunteer. The perception of the needs in each community as identified by the Citizen Advisory Bureaus will determine the design for the delivery of services in Great Britain. Bridged from one service to another, sustained by people who care, personally, families will solve their own problems with help, together, not by being torn asunder for special services. Volunteers know persons as members of a family and community. Surrogate relationships, nurturing relationships from volunteers, and above all the ombudsman make certain that there are services to reach those who need them.

It seems to me that the VACs can keep the agencies in a town person-centered rather than organization-centered. They can look at services to determine whether they are scheduled for optimum service or staff convenience. They can look at the goals of the agency, both hidden and explicit in its legal basis, in terms of its relevance to current conditions. Most local YWCA's, which are dear to my heart, have moved quickly into changing patterns of service. But I'll bet if you took a head count you could still find hat-making classes in some, because there is a volunteer there who likes to teach hat making! A function of the local VAC, then, is to keep that volunteer learning to do something that is going to have more meaning to people than making hats in this day and age. Keeping agencies person-centered is going to keep them from passing the buck, from being much more preoccupied with interpreting what they're not set up to do than with simply doing what they are set up to do. The VACs, by being fairly neutral, will be able to develop more insight and new goals.

Basic to the British plan, which I find exciting, is the principle of geographic justice. We talk a lot about economic justice and social justice, and this means both of those things. But most of all it means, how am I handicapped because of where I am, where I have to live, how far it is to where I am going to be able to work. A lot of our programs are peachy, but they're just in the wrong place. If there's any one universal problem in volunteering, it's transportation. The VACs have a real contribution to make in meeting transportation needs of volunteers, of looking at services from this standpoint, of making it possible for the two to get together.

Another skill the VAC is also going to have to develop in leadership people is the skill of consultation, both in volunteers and staff. But we must develop skills so people can look at their community services, not telling other people what to do, but helping people discover what to do for themselves, reconciling what they think they want with what consultants see they need, because these are not always the same. How are we going to help volunteers in the transition from service to adminstrative roles, to represent us in regional and national perspective. There is very little help given about this. A trap we often fall into at a meeting such as this, is to share our headaches about our own bailiwick instead of listening for ideas and options and solutions. (I hope in the discussion groups here we can avoid that pitfall, and I'm sure with a group at this level we can.)

Summarizing the challenges then, I want the VACs to enlist and help motivate more *different* people as volunteers. If volunteering is a basic human right, then how do we find ways for all humans who want to serve, who would be benefited from serving, to find a place to serve? How do we make our opportunities visible? How do we stimulate trust in volunteers and create a climate in which the new kind of "rescue fantasy" that volunteers are having today, when they spontaneously volunteer, can be preserved, because this is a strong motivating force? How can we persuade staff to let volunteers become *really involved* so that they *know* that they are effective? How can we coordinate the transportation that is available? I lived overseas at one time and gasoline was so expensive that we all filled our cars with people before we moved. I still feel guilty riding around in a car by myself. What can we do to fill up our cars with people who need to get to the other place? What can we do about insurance? What can we do to be certain that public transportation meets public needs and not only the needs of the companies running it?

I see the VAC as kind of a hub of activities, not an umbrella, but a place where relationships will intersect in a community, and a catalyst for all sorts of the adhocracies we were talking about.

I think there are going to be some problems which we might as well face squarely. One is how are we going to overcome the employment agency image? Very exciting is the possibility of tapping computerization for pin point recruitment from a skills bank, which has tremendous possibilities. We're all a little wary that we will be mechanized and not people-centered, and it's up to us how we use this new power. The Isaiah volunteers have identified over 4,000 roles for volunteers in the Philadelphia area and they have a tremendous number of persons who have filled out a blank and have been referred to the agency that needs their specific skills. This community-wide skills inventory is provided by Sun Oil, one of the major industries in the Philadelphia area, which lends its computers on Sundays.

Not unrelated is our problem about the numbers game. We don't really want to be evaluated on the basis of a number of hours of service we have been able to produce with the number of volunteers we have referred to a place. We have a function that goes way beyond this, but we still need some yardstick, and we musn't throw the baby out with the bath water. The volunteers in our New York State system of the Department of Mental Hygiene have been doing fabulous things for individual patients. We have tried in our reporting to show the qualities volunteers contribute. We recruit through helping people to imagine themselves doing some of these things. But when our budget was cut drastically, it was our numbers that made the difference. Post-legislative special provisions were made because we could say that we had more than a million dollars worth of time contributed by our volunteers, on a minimum wage basis. But we try to keep the numbers as broad as that, because we all have times when we need to escape into something that's quite technical and absorbing when we're up tight, and some administrators spend their whole time counting hours, and they just don't get around to doing anything else. There is a fine line there!

I think we need to recognize that under specialized services there are loyalties. We used to laugh ruefully in the Girl Scouts about the volunteers who "took the green veil," who were really afraid to be identified with any other agency for fear of being perceived as disloyal. (I remember I took a PTA job one time, and I was clobbered by telephone because people were afraid I was going to give up my Girl Scout Troop.) I hope the VACs can help extricate staff and volunteers from this constraint. I hope, too, that we will establish the need for paid help in VAC offices. This sounds like an awfully petty thing, but a lot of leadership in the field of voluntarism is bottled up doing paper work, because the community assumes that volunteers should do the steno and record keeping at the office. Part of the package for real leadership of a VAC will mean that office services will be considered legitimate administrative costs, and we won't have to worry about inappropriate use of leadership time and talents!

Most of all, when we think of the VAC as a hub, let's see it as a way of cutting diagonally through the strata of society, of throwing people together so they find their commonality as they won't have any other opportunity to do in the community. Each comes to appreciate the strength of the other, and together they create something new and valuable out of what may have been old hat to some but new to other people of different backgrounds. How many times in discussion groups which are organized in this diagonal cut, people say, "Why, I never knew that about our town, or about an agency, or about a group which might be willing to serve." There are tremendous untapped sources of volunteers with strengths for communities, who are unaware of the fact that they're needed. There's a rich potential in working together beyond the value of individual efforts. I would remind you of what Mr. Branch said last night, that they are so busy solving the problems in Atlanta that they don't have time for pettiness. This is a tip for us all. If our emphasis is on the need and working out a way to meet it, we're not going to have time to be petty about whose prerogatives are being altered. Nothing ventured, nothing gained!

Mr. Sheldon spoke of process as the heart of the Voluntary Action Center and the key to the approach that the Center uses in the community. The roles that the VACs develop will tap all kinds of human potential, and methods will be found that are tailored to each community. Chris Mould reminded us that there will be resources available in over 1,000 categories of Federal programs, but we've got to know where we're at and what we need before we ask.

I hope we won't put a ceiling on what we ask or on what we see as a potential. I hope we won't think that we have to go through all of the trauma of incorporating and building a structure which in turn is frozen, to meet new needs for new services, but that the old and the new will be able to work together on temporary bases, intensively on a chosen need. We know this about volunteers, we know this about needs: Many problems can be solved if we all pay attention to them. Many volunteers will serve on a time-limited commitment where they can see that they're the person who is needed. Insure a wide range of representation in that problem solving. We're going to have some strange and wonderful adhocracies but they will find better solutions than ever. One of the best

coordinators of volunteers I know had with her, at the AAVSC
meetings in Philadelphia recently, a beautiful poster. It's my
challenge to you! It said, "Only he who attempts the absurd
accomplishes the impossible."

5

Needed: Professional Competence For Volunteer Administration

The concept of a generic profession for volunteer administration may seem esoteric, but my experience as volunteer, as staff member and in giving leadership to volunteer programming has convinced me it is imperative to consider the possibility of staff development to levels of competence and influence which are unquestionably at the professional level. The NCVA encourages the development of local Voluntary Action Centers to insure the health of voluntarism in our democracy, but without people able to give continuous and creative paid leadership the goals are hollow.

Most of the people now employed in many fields to administer volunteer programs work quite alone or with very few associates who understand what conflicting pressures can build up. To survive, volunteer administrators (usually called directors or coordinators) must tread a fine line between administrative pressures to pick up a miscellany of tasks with community relations aspects and community pressures to serve the purposes of individuals or groups. Clarity about values and great skill are required to bring all goals into congruence with the ideal of service to meet the real needs of persons for whom the services are intended. An organized profession could back up lonely practitioners when pressures mount from either their organization setting or community.

A profession could be developed which would bridge between fields of practice and transcend the demands of daily practice with a focus on human needs, open options for mobility for its members on a career lattice, rather than limit them to a one-track ladder, and support them when besieged in struggles which obscure the persons who may be probationer, patient, client, committee member or advocate as consumers of their services.

The creation of a profession is a complex process involving grandfathering in many persons from a variety of disciplines and life experiences. Each individual should have appropriate opportunities for filling his gaps in the knowledge and skills required for effective practice. This profession has unique personal qualifications required which loom even more essential than academic credentials. As an adult educator I have faith that people can change attitudes and develop competencies at all ages or levels. Appropriate learning constantly to combat obsolescence of past learnings for widely different persons requires a complex curriculum development process.

Analysis of the theoretical and philosophical basis must come at an early stage. Otherwise training is likely to be limited to meeting urgent but recurring needs for operational demands. I believe if we give people at every educational level understanding of the "why's", the "how-to's" come more easily. Without a value system of "why's" administrative decisions are subject to whim and personal idiosyncracy to a devastating degree, even while technical knowledge is improved.

We need professionals, not mere technicians, people with wide and forward vision, to coordinate otherwise unrelated factors into a functioning administrative whole.

Without "why's" administrative decisions as to procedures and budgets may be whimsical and thus difficult to interpret. Granting the urgent need for practical techniques by people now in the jobs, my plea for curriculum development is to provide a variety of appropriate learning opportunities for persons of widely varying backgrounds on a continuing education basis. No education today is complete: our ideas are often soon obsolete with the changing matrix in which we carry complex responsibilities. We all need renewal and inspiration as well as technical know-how for doing the basic "housekeeping" so we can live comfortably in our jobs. Curriculum for specific fields is very important, too. But there are basic human values and administrative principles which are always needed.

I see the National Center for Voluntary Action as a catalyst in curriculum development for cross fertilization between fields of volunteer administration practice. Just as the neutral volunteer influences an interdisciplinary team, NCVA can help organizations remain person-centered. The NCVA would not necessarily administer learning opportunities needed, but could carry on some innovative activities as demonstrations and provide some basic education for the new VAC leadership, both staff and volunteer.

Transcendent neutrality could stimulate interest in universal need for a generic profession, and influence academic and informal adult education agencies to provide opportunities for credit and noncredit, short-term and full credentialling academic programs.

The following *Recommendations* formulated by a discussion group at the 1972 Boulder conference on curriculum require supplementary information, keyed to the outline attached:

RECOMMENDATIONS

Formulated by Harriet Naylor

from input received at the

CONFERENCE OF COLLEGE CURRICULA

for the

LEADERSHIP OF HUMAN SERVICE

VOLUNTEER PROGRAMS

National Information Center on

Volunteerism

I.   There is a nationwide need for *leadership* in establishing volunteer administration as a profession, requisites of which are:

    A. an organization in which all persons in the field may have membership

    B. identification of a basic body of knowledge needed

    C. educational curriculum, embodying essential accumulated knowledge, for those desiring to enter the volunteer administration profession and for those in practice desiring to improve their knowledge and skills

D. a medium for disseminating information about openings, for persons seeking employment in the field

E. a code of ethics and standards for certification

F. a journal for sharing information about theory and practice

II. There is a need for continuing *communication* of the values of voluntarism and volunteer service to a variety of audiences:

A. general public

B. educational institutions

C. governmental bodies

D. volunteers themselves

E. allied professions

F. Civil Service and credentialling bodies (especially re values of volunteer experience)

III. There is continuing need for *storage and retrieval* of information about developments in the field of practice:

A. Program ideas

B. Resources

1. reference materials
2. people as consultants
3. organizations as providers of technical assistance
4. teaching materials

IV. There is need for *funding* educational opportunities on an in-individual scholarship as well as program grant basis, to develop a wide variety of educational programs to meet a wide spectrum of learning needs!

I. A. Leadership is now being exerted by at least four national organizations, the National Information Center on Volunteers in Courts, the American Association of Volunteer Service Coordinators, the Association of Volunteer Bureaus of America, and the Society Directors for Volunteer Services. The latter membership organizations, all are related to specific fields with associate memberships for persons in other fields. It seems unlikely or unnecessary that any one would become an "umbrella", but the strengths and experience of each should be maintained and tapped. The impetus generated by the Court Volunteer movement for a guild for volunteers is likely to be necessary unless the volunteer administrator profession builds up ways for volunteers to participate in the determination of program service objectives and delivery patterns. The consumer revolution could mean adversaries, but volunteers within the system could mean allies, if volunteers have good staff partnership experiences. To me, this is an essential function of the Voluntary Action Center at national and especially at local levels, where individual advocates are powerless or need to find allies.

B.&C. The AVBA and the AAVSC have done nationwide surveys of learning needs which should be used in identifying the basic learning needed, and the SDVS has the great resources of the American Hospital Association studies on tap, and all three have active, interested education committees, all of whom contributed to the Boulder conference. The NCVA Clearinghouse has a listing of reported events.

D.   All three have newsletters and could expand their use for personnel exchange.

E.   To my knowledge only one of the organizations, the AAVSC, has evolved a code of ethics and has a certification procedure. The AVBA has defined such a process for Volunteer Bureaus, but not for individual professional workers.

F.   Each newsletter carries some information about theory and practice. VOLUNTEER ADMINISTRATION published by Northeast University has potential for becoming a professional journal.

II.   The NCVA through the Clearinghouse and Communications activities is already taking a lead communicating to many audiences and could expand as needed. There are special informational and attitude changes needed by the allied professions for persons trained before volunteering changed its scope and depth, or threatened by myths and misunderstandings of the volunteer potential.

III.   The Clearinghouse is already recognized as the logical central repository for information on program ideas, resources, references and consultation possibilities.

IV.   Funding, an ever-present problem, might be handled nationally by a scholarship committee on a project basis by the NCVA for individuals or by constituent groups, since many national agencies already have scholarship programs.

As the National Center with full staff and committees swings into gear, I hope serious thought will be given by all to the need for qualified, inspired and inspiring staff leadership for all fields where volunteers serve. The proposed regional events to follow up the Atlanta meeting offer an opportunity to consult local people as a normative model, which I would hope local Voluntary Action Centers will replicate when the delegate gets back home.

What YOU bring to

Think about what the work involves, and what you already know and can do, why you were selected. Put + and why in those boxes where you feel prepared.
Now, honestly, where do you feel unprepared, and where would you welcome help through training? Put a - there and note what you need to learn.

The Work to be done:	Gathering and Analysing	Goal setting	Planning & Budgeting	Organizing & Scheduling	Delegating & Supervising	Coordinating & Communicating	Evaluating	Reporting
Knowledge & Awareness								
Skills in process								
Feelings about the process: likes & dislikes, loyalties & prejudices								
Connections with organizations & individuals								
Personal goals & objectives								
Significant experience								
Ideals—how you think it ought to be, what you will be shooting for								

6

ADMINISTRATION FOR SERVICES OF OLDER VOLUNTEERS

Professional administration for services involving older persons as volunteers requires recognition of myths which people believe about aging and of other real differences which deserve special consideration. The process of matching skills to special needs is especially challenging because developmental differences become more marked over the human life-span. Some physical slowing down and loss of perceptual acuities must be recognized, but attendance and retention records for older volunteers show greater reliability than for younger ones! Perhaps volunteering has heightened meaning when one's earning and child rearing days are over. Individualizing each volunteer to maximize his potential and avoiding stereotyping or untested assumptions are just as important for older persons as for any other volunteer. It is simply more costly to short circuit the process because older persons are likely to have undisclosed strengths and wisdom which they have come to underestimate because of their experience in having been excluded from participation and function in American social life. New roles as volunteers meet the very human and basic need to be needed.

Staff attitudes from the top administrator on down set the climate which determines the effectiveness of all volunteer services. Staff who appreciate and welcome older volunteers are providing a good preventive service for them in keeping them highly motivated and active and developing a self-concept of a needed participant in society. Inter-staff relationships involving the Coordinator of Volunteer Services and other employees are sometimes very complex in the large institutional settings which need volunteers the most. In a very small program responsibilities are for direct supervision of volunteers in their activities. Larger settings demand a division of responsibility which highlights the contrast of administrative tasks for the Coordinator of Volunteer Services and supervisory tasks carried by the staff "in the front line."

Success with staff is diluted by every level of supervision through which we must work in dealing with those with whom we do not come in direct contact. The dynamics are sometimes complicated by the existence of staff who run activities for a Senior Citizen's Center. Leadership by the Coordinator of Volunteer Services means that all of the staff members are brought to see the congruency of their objectives toward a shared goal. Meeting the needs of older volunteers, of the client or target population and of all of the employees involved means that mutual accountability and communication patterns are essential. Periodic program review avoids having problems grow out of control. Line staff can perceive volunteers as much needed manpower, and Senior Center Directors can perceive volunteering as a very valuable program activity for older persons. Each staff member must be helped to realize that this can best be achieved through collaboration with the other staff involved in the Senior Volunteer program.

Because so many older persons are managing on limited and fixed incomes, their need for enabling funding is determinant in recruiting. To be assured of carfare and a hot lunch is a real inducement and has been known to be the original motivation to service for persons who feel deprived of some amenities with inflation pressures on their retired life-style.

The right of choice is dear to volunteer and staff members alike. Therefore both should have a voice in the design of an assignment and the contract to carry it out. We need constantly to look for beginning level assignments for older persons in which they can gain confidence and enjoy their work. The recruitment process must be much more active and reassuring than with many other volunteers. The SERVE program which became the pattern for

RSVP has proved the importance of a tour of many possible volunteer opportunities before a choice is made. Older persons should be shown needs for volunteers which they could visualize themselves meeting.

The orientation to a program is essential but should be as individualized as possible. Many older persons are apprehensive about any class-room-like atmosphere, but can learn very well in an informal group situation which is not called training. Each volunteer should know at the outset the person to whom he reports and those to whom he can turn for help if he should need it.

Older volunteers may make a very limited commitment at first, but frequently indicate willingness to serve many more hours than the original contract. They may discover other roles they would like to take, and for these reasons a periodic review with the Coordinator of Volunteer Services should take place. Again a range of choice should be opened for eveyone so that there is no loss of face if someone wants to make a change, either the staff member or the volunteer. Often surprising new talents are discovered and the older volunteer gains great satisfaction from realizing that he can learn "new tricks." The older volunteers in the SERVE program were so enthusiastic about their experiences that instead of having a recognition of their own, they gave a party and gave awards to the staff who had made their volunteer work possible. An analysis of the SERVE*experience indicates that staff collaboration is essential and that the group identity of the older volunteers as "SERVE volunteers" had a high retention value. Like all volunteers, the older volunteer appreciates being treated as an unpaid staff member whose point of view is important and whose ideas are welcomed. Thus a program review will contain many valuable insights from the volunteer as he perceives the impact of services upon the client. It is essential to build a structure which provides access to program development and goal setting for the volunteer. He needs to realize that his observations and innovated ideas are valuable and will be given serious consideration in developing policy.

Many older volunteers feel very sorry that they did not know the joy of volunteering earlier in life. They become advocates for the

*Seniors, Enrich Retirement in Volunteer Experience, Community Service Society of New York City.

service in which they work and for the staff with whom they work. Not all older persons will choose a one-to-one relationship with a client, but those who do become very articulate advocates for their client. Recognition, for them, comes from the client himself and his progress in the program.

Administration has been defined as the accomplishment of goals through the efforts of other persons. When older persons are entitled as volunteers, their efforts can make a tremendous difference in the lives of the people with whom they work. Coordination of volunteer services then means that each older volunteer is placed where he can use his unique knowledge and skills and where he enjoys working. As RSVP spreads across the United States, the administration of programs involving older volunteers will tap the greatest unused pool of manpower we have in the United States today. It is up to us to find ways for everybody to help somebody!

7

Volunteers in Government

Government *needs* volunteers! Caught between budget slashes and pressure from special interest groups and more demanding customers, government agencies need all the help they can get! Volunteers are the concerned people all around us who are just waiting to be told where they are needed. After a recent television program about patient needs in a state school for the mentally retarded, more than a thousand offers of help were received, some from several hundred miles away. Most of those people offered to come in to feed severely handicapped residents, or to take them out for walks—things the staff, shorthanded by a job freeze, would never have time to do, even though they probably would like to. Some of those thousand live too far away to volunteer at that state school, but they may live near you. Do they know what kinds of help *you* could use? Have you ever stopped to think of a volunteer when unmet needs are reported to you as a public administrator?

We know from recent studies that there is less than a 60% chance you did consider calling volunteers if you work in the field of rehabilitation services. (1) If you are in social welfare, law, fiscal management, personnel administration, employment counseling or correction, the chances are likely to be much less. (2) If you're in housing, courts or corrections; (3) health or mental health, you have a better chance. (4) Every one of these critical governmental services is chronically short staffed and often under attack from newspapers and consumers. Experts in many fields deplore dehumanizing practices and inadequate

Presented at the American Society of Public Administrators conference March 23, 1972 New York City.

provisions for rehabilitation due to manpower shortages. Volunteers can provide auxiliary manpower. Besides the priceless time and effort they give for free, they bring a humanitarian concern that gets through to patients or prisoners or welfare clients. Often the volunteer is the first person they have talked to for a long time who comes because he *wants* to listen to them, not because he is *paid* to. It makes a difference in how people feel about themselves to have a friend who wants to listen. New hope stirs and apathy changes to ability to make better use of the paid professional help available, too.

The Bureau of Labor Statistics lists very few occupations whose work could not be strengthened or extended by complementary volunteer efforts. Time invested inducting and training volunteers is returned many times over, multiplied by the work that they can do. For example, one speech therapist could serve almost 300 in residence when the volunteers there were taught to handle speech practice sessions, one-to-one. The speech therapist could then devote her time to diagnosis and prescription which only she was qualified to do. If she had been responsible for the time-consuming follow-through, she would have been able to serve about ten a week.

The multiplier effect of using volunteers applies to many disciplines which are in short supply. They are the ones trained in and responsible for a particular function, who should advise what volunteers could be assigned to do within it. The administrator with their advice can identify and group into attractive jobs certain volunteer responsibilities which will make the efforts of paid staff more effective and widen the span of influence for each highly skilled worker. The levels of skills required in these volunteer responsibilities can run the gamut from simple, entry level tasks to technically complex responsibilities for fully qualified professionals. Some professionals choose practice without pay for a variety of reasons: frustrating limits in their paid jobs, early retirement or transcendent obligations such as those of the mother of small children who wants to keep up her skills and talk adult-talk sometimes, but can't take a job. As volunteers, they are professionally accountable to the clients of the service, and work cooperatively

with the paid staff assigned to induct and train them in the
policies and ground rules of that work setting. Other professionals
prefer volunteering to be totally different from their life work.

Many people want to get out of a rut and meet new kinds
of people. Most frequently volunteers are laymen in the field to
which they are assigned, and they all want to do something
constructive for someone else. Spontaneity, common sense,
warmth and basic living skills are invaluable assets in most
programs. A volunteer friend with an accurate empathetic
ear, who knows the community can tap its resources for a job
and a place to live for an ex-prisoner or a convalescent.
With such help, returnees can be bridged into the real
world which changes too fast even for those of us who haven't
left. With volunteer support they stand a better chance of
making it.

Volunteers work in groups, too, in the public services.
Clubs take on short, intensive projects, such as furnishing
an apartment for a burned-out welfare family. A sustained
project might be a block-by-block information service about local
services, like CIO-AFL community service volunteers, or keeping
track of housing and nursing home vacancies so that social
workers with clients needing transfer don't have to start
from scratch to find a place. Amateur groups armed with basic
criteria can do the initial legwork needed in home-finding
for children or convalescents, or follow-up on longitudinal
research projects, or sustain patterning for the exhausted family
of a brain-damaged child. Groups combine forces voluntarily,
too, such as the JC's who provide transportation for students from
campus to the places where they volunteer in town. Incidentally,
students make fabulous volunteers. With their idealism and
enthusiasm, they don't believe that something can't be done, so
they go ahead and do it! Older persons bring great wisdom as
volunteers which otherwise might be wasted.

Volunteers come in all ages and kinds of people. When they
volunteer as a group, there are added retention factors built
in: peer expectations and the group reputation bolster continued
interest. (5) The basic human group, the family, is volunteering
too. Offering a respite to another family by taking a senior

member or a hyperactive or retarded child into their own
home for a visit may mean that that family can carry on
afterwards, refreshed and enabled to postpone or avoid institutionalization. Old-fashioned neighborliness, for the people who
need it most! In one family visiting program, an 8-year-
old retarded child was taught to speak by two little boys
in a family she was visiting. Imagine the commitment to
volunteering they will have now that their faith in their
"rescue fantasy" has been justified! Observers concerned about
eroding family life see family volunteering as a counter force.
The National Center for Voluntary Action has set high priority
on developing volunteer services for aging persons in their own
homes or places of residence as alternatives to institutional care.

Experience with the war on poverty has taught that the
victim of an economic or social problem can make a special,
valuable contribution as a volunteer working with fellow victims.
He has a ring of authenticity which makes him communicate
more persuasively than highly technical advisors. Now mental
health, physical health, drug abuse and correctional programs are
training their clients as volunteers, too. Where people must
be herded individualization becomes impossible. Pairing volunteers
with patients or inmates helps each to retain his identity and
to respond to treatment or opportunities in his own way.

The Ribicoff bill (Sen. 1212) died in committee last year,
but the idea of citizen advocates to facilitate use of services
is catching on in many other fields. Volunteers can help a
family through the community maze of intake requirements and
territorial jurisdictions to secure appropriate services. Volunteer
transportation pools and escort services can save hours of staff
time. The volunteer describing a service to a potential user
is credible because he *is* a volunteer, and doubly so if
he himself has used the service, too. Who could do this out
of your target group for his fellows?

Experiments have proved the value of mass media recruiting,
TV, radio, newspapers, billboards, community bulletin boards.
We are finding that these media produce young, employed
persons, not traditional middle class housewives who tend to recruit
each other. For residential services, young employed persons are

ideal volunteers because they are available evenings and weekends, when employed staff like to be off. By staggering staff to facilitate volunteer services, residential program services can be expanded into evening and free time of resident populations, not just 9 to 5. A good way to avoid weekend sag, as well. The National Center for Voluntary Action is going to sponsor a nationwide mass media campaign for volunteers. Are you ready to use the time and talents of young employed persons as volunteers? To train and supervise them? If you have to turn them away, what will it do to your agency reputation?

Recruitment is never a problem where volunteers are appreciated and find interesting important work to do. Being ready for volunteers means having a variety of jobs defined, clients willing to try having volunteers, staff ready to get them started, and supervise their work. Priority of time and effort demands strong support from the top. Public administrators have to make it clear that this is the route to rewards in the organization; staff members must plan ways volunteers could be useful, to design orientation and training opportunities, and set up schedules which put client needs first and accommodate staff needs, too, both paid and unpaid. Among unpaid volunteers there are likely to be some who will need transportation money, or lunch money if assignments are likely to stretch over a meal time. The ACTION Retired Senior Volunteer Program now to be administered through each state Office for Aging, has built in provision for senior volunteers, which established the principle that such provision is a legitimate administrative expense. Now we should extend such provisions to *all* volunteers who need expense money to be able to serve.

Many agencies fail to realize additional fringe benefits which are possible when an agency uses volunteer manpower for public relations and program development. Because volunteers come into a program with a variety of memberships and identities they become emissaries of the agency in their churches, clubs and neighborhoods, building public sympathy and support for its goals and programs among their relatives and friends because they believe in what they are doing. Because they are unpaid, they have seen firsthand, they have a special ring of authenticity. Volunteering is training ground for agency program needs, speakers' bureaus, trainers, recruiters, resource mobilizers and they can say things about salary levels and program values that paid staff would find hard to say without being vulnerable to charges of self-interest. Yet right now, with so many irrational pennywise, pound foolish budget cuts due to gross misunderstanding of what public agencies are trying to do, ironically volunteers are still underestimated and underutilized as interpreters for the agencies, with access to many sources for manpower and for public support for governmental services.

Public agency administrators have not enlisted volunteers as agency defenders, possibly because they have been preoccupied with the very problems volunteers could help them solve. As agency staffs plan and operate services, experienced, informed volunteers have a unique perspective to contribute. Neutral between consumers and providers, volunteers assess the impact of services in humane, nontechnical terms, spotting gaps, judge effectiveness and report realities or changing conditions on behalf of less articulate consumers. Aware of local resources through their connections in the community, volunteers can often mobilize support and materials for budgets and for extra-budget provisions which enrich and reinforce programs.

Governmental tax-supported agencies must serve all who suffer the need defined in their laws and regulations. Voluntary contributor-supported agencies are expected to concentrate on special needs and to demonstrate new ways to translate their democratic ideals into action. Ambiguities abound, as Elizabeth Wickenden and the United Way of America have pointed out; it is increasingly difficult to distinguish the "public sector" from the "voluntary sector" and both from the "private for profit sector" which traditionally included business, industry and organized labor. Rooted in Peter Drucker's concept of *reprivatization* is an accelerating trend toward competition for public funds for the purchase of services by government from the voluntary and private organizations, either on a fee basis or by project grants. Under the 1967 Harris Amendment to the Social Security Act, slowly being implemented, services can be purchased by government from voluntary agencies and the use of volunteers is mandated for public assistance and child welfare programs which involve federal reimbursement.* A detailed review "Citizen Participation in Federal Programs" available from the Association of Voluntary Action Scholars, shows the burgeoning opportunities. At the state level, two have fulltime overall volunteer services leadership, Washington and Illinois, while Massachusetts, New York, Delaware and many others are in the process of developing statewide coordination of citizen efforts, or attempting it as a part-time beyond-the-job activity. Mrs. Josephine Oblinger, Executive Director of Governor Ogilvie's Committee on Voluntary Action, when initiating February as "Voluntary Action Month", gave a breakdown of the number of volunteers and the formidable number of dollars saved the State of Illinois government by volunteer services: In the Department of Mental Health, 16,191 volunteers gave 310,654 manhours, $497,046 saved at minimum wage rates; Department of Conservation; 3,714 estimated $65,000; Civil Defense: 35,000 volunteers, uncounted hours; Cook County Department of Public Aid: 14,040 manhours at $3.18 per hour, $44,647; Public Health: 17 volunteers, 2,510 manhours, $4,016; 4510 students at 56 schools with 231 volunteer programs gave 541,200 manhours saved $865,920 at minimum wage rates. The real manhour value is impossible to pinpoint precisely. The only fact which is certain is that the recorded figures must be minimal. The true value has no dollar sign, although there are tremendous long-range savings in preventing imprisonment, reducing recidivision, or habilitating the handicapped to maintain themselves as productive taxpayers in the community. We do know that care in residential facilities costs many thousands of dollars per person per year, so that every human being who can be salvaged will be a contributing member of society rather than a drain on its assets.

---

* Title XVI amended this requirement in continental USA by substituting Supplementary Security Income (SSI) for the blind, aged and permanently disabled in continental USA effective Jan. 1, 1974.

Title XX, effective Oct. 1, 1975, eliminated the child welfare mandate but suggests that state plans include private as well as public agencies, and volunteers in the delivery of services.

Government, voluntary and the private sector are inextricably inter-dependent and each has a real stake in the quality of life in American communities. The "private sector" subsidizes and participates voluntarily because corporations and labor unions like individuals, realize the importance of being givers as well as receivers to one's community. Job Corps and Manpower Training programs depend on all three sectors. Zerox loans executives and the Prudential Insurance Company line employees, matching hour for hour given, released time for volunteering. Other employers are following their lead. In New York City there is an Association of Directors of Volunteers—paid full time— who place employees from their companies in the community as volunteers.

As George Meany, President of AFL-CIO, stated union policy in the NCVA Newsletter recently, "And only strong voluntary organizations of determined free men and women can prevent the strong temptations of equally determined men on horseback to run our lives down in the mill and in the mine, in the neighborhood and in the nation. That's what the labor movement is all about—a voluntary organization of free men and women cooperating with other voluntary organizations of free men and women for a more representative, a more responsive and more responsible society. The heart of the labor movement is the volunteer worker, and its best expression is in community service."

The National Center for Voluntary Action is encouraging individually tailored local Voluntary Action Centers across the country to develop *receiving systems*, as well as delivery systems for human services. As catalyst, VAC's convene forums on special needs for staff, administrators, clients, volunteers, media, clubs and organizations who want to "do good". The VAC helps them work out ways to do good better. These volunteer information and referral centers become a resource for public administrators, with information on services, volunteers, resources and program impact feedback.

The more government agencies participate in the developmental process for VAC's, the more likely their local VAC services will be to take useful form and consideration for public agency priorities. Supporting and nurturing leadership potential in the community, the VAC's will be able to mobilize knowledgeable volunteers (who may have come up through the ranks) citizen advisory committees and comprehensive community planning assignments. Public agencies will have to move positively to attract volunteers.

The competition for able persons is keen, although some public services seem increasingly to welcome volunteers. Volunteers are valuable personnel who deserve responsible support. The key to agency volunteer administration is the staff specifically assigned to build up a sound coordinated operating pattern for volunteer job development, recruiting, orientation and training, record keeping and communicating with the agency's various public and staff leaders. A good way to insure competency in volunteer administraton is employment of a Certified Volunteer Coordinator—certified by the Association of Administrators of Volunteer Services. In the job, the CVC needs access to the overall program planning process with firm administrative support stressing the values of having volunteers.

The Joint Commission on Accreditation with the AAVS has explicit standards for mental health and retardation. In practical terms these should mean a pleasant accessible office with adequate clerical help and telephone coverage. The tone of the ideal organization reflects administrator attitudes which McGregor described as trusting people and encouraging creativity, innovation and quick, appropriate response to expressions of need and changing conditions, without inflexible, binding regulations. Volunteer administration takes professional level abilities to keep on top of the dynamics of inter-staff and community relations, to accept, deploy and acknowledge contributions and keep everyone happily productive. Personality factors are more important than skills, the major one being openness to new ideas—the ability to scan community and agency for forecast, and to match volunteers to needs, to communicate well to many different persons, to teach; to help other staff to supervise, to record and retrieve information; to confederate in adhocracies and to disband them when no longer needed, and to evaluate the impact of volunteers on the program as the basis for future planning.

According to David C. Knapp, Dean of the New York State College of Human Ecology at Cornell, we have to "make social sense out of many unrelated research and programmatic endeavors—by testing new and alternative social arrangements for improving human welfare—by government-university cooperation." Volunteers, the private sector and voluntarism offer time, skills and resources to apply in the efforts of government. Knapp really challenges public administrators when he goes on to say: "Most contemporary human problems are as Charles Lindbloom has suggested 'synthetic' not because they are unreal, but because they are syntheses of many interrelated problems. Poverty—rural or urban—is not a single problem, for example, but many problems bound into one. Its alleviation will be attained only if these interconnected problems can be tackled more or less simultaneously."

Voluntary, governmental and private sector administrators are needed. ASPA has a crucial responsibility to bring the public administrators into the game!

ASPA Conference Footnotes:

1. *Volunteering in Rehabilitation Facilities* Goodwill Industries of America, Inc. 9200 Wisconsin Ave., Washington, D.C., 20014

2. *Volunteers in New York State Government* survey by the Governor's Interdepartmental Committee on Volunteers, 1970

3. See the reports of the National Information Service on Volunteers in Courts and Corrections. P.O. Box 2150, Boulder Springs, Colorado, 80302

4. *People Helping People* U.S. News and World Report Washington, D.C., 1971

5. Report on the S.E.R.V.E. program, model for RSVP legislation in the Title VI, Older American Act, Community Service Society of New York, 1971, winner of the NCVA group service award for 1972.

6. Wickenden, Elizabeth, "Purchase of Care and Services:" Effect on Voluntary Agencies, *Proceedings, Milwaukee Institute.* University of Wisconsin School of Social Welfare, July 1970.

7. Coley, Hamp, *Expanding Local Service Programs Through Government Purchase of Services,* United Way of America 1972.

8. Speigel, Hans, B. C., of C.U.N.Y., "*Citizen Participation in Federal Programs: A Review*". Monograph No. 1, 1971, *Journal of Voluntary Action Research* Room 300, 1507 M Street, N. W., Washington, D.C., 20005

9. Adopted from Michael, Donald N., "Influencing Public Policy, the Changing Roles of Voluntary Associations", Journal of Current Social Issues, Autumn '71.

8

The Volunteer Option
in Retirement

. . . a volunteer assignment is so valuable for the volunteer,
that volunteering ought to be a basic human right . . .
Every person should have this option, because it's just as natural
to want to help other people as it is to feel the power of sex or hunger
drives, which get a lot more attention.

Even though we have been very active in our work life, in retirement we tend to become isolated, unless we keep a network of
connections with other people. Volunteering is an excellent way to
do that.

Everybody looks at human problems in one of four ways:
—"That's your problem, not mine."
—"People came from outside and *made* the problem."
—"There is no problem; what's everybody talking about?"
—"Your problem is my problem."
We want to be perceived by our fellow men as persons responsive
to human needs. All of us care about some causes that are important, basic human problems which concern us. Joining in a movement helps us feel that there can be counter-forces in our society
today. We can be part of the solution . . . not just part of the
problem . . .

This is a good time in history to be considering volunteering in
retirement, because the "volunteer explosion" is on. It is a good idea
to do some volunteer work before retirement, as Toffler recom-
mended in "Future Shock." Take a foray into the future patterns
beforehand to test different patterns so that when you make a drastic
change, you have already been there.

What you might do is up to you. It is said, "What you are is God's gift to you; what you make of yourself is your gift to God." What you make of yourself as a volunteer means meeting some of your own deepest needs for new roles and relationships, as well as meeting needs of others. When we think about volunteering, we think of it as giving . . . and this is true. What we give is particularly valuable because it is a gift of self. But most volunteers say they get far more than they give. People who are thinking about volunteering often don't realize what it will mean to them as persons, besides a chance to use the skills and abilities they have.

Volunteering has many choices. You may want to volunteer as an individual person and just go out on your own. You may want to work with staff partners doing some of the things that the staff lack time and resources to do in an existing agency. You may want to devise a group project. A family can volunteer, opening their home or sharing a treat.

Opportunities are endless for the individual volunteer. They are needed in research—particularly longitudinal studies . . . consumer services . . . in welfare services—lifting some of the responsibility for the problems from the shoulders of the social worker to those of the layman and marshalling resources not open to either clients or social workers. There is a growing need for staff assistants as teacher aides, case aides, recreation helpers . . . a place for every skill, every talent, every offer of friendship. In administration there is a great need for board members who can work cooperatively with the many kinds of leadership emerging in our beleagured cities, or interpret needs, or help in the raising and in the managing of agency monies.

In an Aerospace Museum in California, senior volunteers can choose from: restoring old aircraft; cataloging a rare collection of aeronautical books, pamphlets, scrapbooks and photographs; making parts which are no longer available, etc. Their enthusiasm keeps most of them working five days a week. This opportunity was made available with the help of a government agency.

Because a School Board in Kentucky was receptive to the premise that the talent and experience of senior citizens could enhance the school experience for high school students, a very successful enrichment and tutorial program has been in operation since 1965.

Specific skills of each volunteer are used in enrichment courses and in specialized help to students selected by their teachers.

The senior volunteer who feels he would make a successful employment counselor can help find his peers jobs in a program in Iowa, or can help obtain pledges for summer jobs for disadvantaged youths in a program in Maryland. This is a highly professional task in which the volunteer works closely with area businessmen and must use sound judgment in placing applicants.

In a program in Massachusetts the senior volunteer is assigned to contact a number of nursing homes to locate bed vacancies, determine levels of care furnished, type of payment accepted, etc. The volunteer also makes follow-up visits to the older people placed.

Serving on a one-to-one basis as a volunteer counselor, the senior citizen in a Washington State Reformatory may teach an inmate a trade, locate job prospects and in other ways smooth the transition between institution and community. The volunteer is also involved in tutoring programs, and even babysitting for young mothers during visiting hours.

In a program in New York older persons reach out to isolated and home-bound elderly, serve through a government-sponsored program as grandparent/parent substitutes, and—in another New York program—befriend and counsel with mothers who either neglect or abuse their children.

Men and women retired from their own active businesses share their expertise and experience through a government-sponsored program with small businessmen who have management and operating problems. The volunteer makes a detailed analysis of the problem and offers a plan to remedy the trouble, continuing the relationship through the critical period.

If the interaction of a group is preferred . . . and the type of "thing" that requires bringing together informed volunteers . . . there are many opportunities available.

A major component of a large senior volunteer program in New York State utilizes the group approach. For this government-sponsored aspect of their program they recruit in groups, and their volunteers serve in groups in a given agency. Regular group discussions provide ongoing in-service training and a mutually beneficial sharing of ideas, experiences, and social interaction.

A craft co-op shop in Missouri depends upon the close cooperation of a group to effect the necessary bookkeeping, sales, policy-making and other chores to run an efficient operation.

Offered to units and chapters of a national organization for retired persons is a tax-aide program operated by older volunteers with services open to all older persons in the community. Local sponsors must meet certain basic requirements to assure success of the program, and are kept up-to-date by the national staff. This same umbrella organization sponsors a program that provides con-sumer information through local affiliates to the general public. This program requires progress reports, recruitment, public relations, follow-up . . . all the responsibilities of a successful business.

A joint effort of a local public library and a government-sponsored program for senior volunteers has helped a Texas library accumu-late a taped history of their area's senior citizens' experiences. Close cooperation within the group insures no duplication in interviewing, and a smooth documentation of the material.

A coalition of old and young in Philadelphia focuses on action to bring about social change for both groups. They are concerned with health care, housing, mass transportation, reforms in Social Security, and the rights of older people. In progress by the group is development of a cooperative non-profit residence for older and younger adults.

Families serving together strengthen their bonds. One family with two young sons took in a retarded girl with an IQ of less than 25. The boys could not believe that any person couldn't talk and never let up stimulating her. After several visits it was found that the younger of the two boys helped her to talk. The retarded child is now considered trainable, which will make a tremendous difference in her life.

Also, volunteer families offer respite to the family of the person they are helping . . . a little time free of responsibility so they can resume their care of a retarded child, a pre-delinquent, an older person . . . refreshed. It is a healthy experience for both families—gratifying to know what has been done to lift everyone to a new level of potential.

9

The Uniqueness of Voluntary Action Centers

Every local Voluntary Action Center is absolutely unique because they are all tailored to the resources and priorities in their given community. Linda Palmer told you what happened in Binghamton, which happens to have a very important resource: A strong and wealthy Junior League committed a great deal of money for the next three years, on a sliding scale basis, to start a Voluntary Action Center, consistent with the Junior League pattern for starting Volunteer Bureaus.

There are some significant differences between traditional Volunteer Bureaus and Voluntary Action Centers and, as I told the people in Binghamton, you don't have to go through all those evolutionary stages. You can start flying in jets. The original Volunteer Bureaus were a membership service to members of organizations like the Junior League and the National Council of Jewish Women as part of their membership patterns. Provisionals had to give community service to become full members. They looked for nice places for their members to serve. They did not assess needs, they assessed the climate for the volunteer, important because a volunteer can walk out at the drop of a hat, but not what we have in mind for the Voluntary Action Center. When I went in as Director of Volunteers for the State Department of Mental Hygiene, I went around to Volunteer Bureaus assuming they were going to be helpful, but some of them said, "We don't serve anything except

Presented at the Chenango County Development Project meeting June 14, 1972 Norwich New York voluntary agencies. We can't supply volunteers for government." They also couldn't supply volunteers for fund raising purposes. It stifles a program if volunteers see a need and can't do anything about it unless somebody else will appropriate some funds. In some cases, it is essential for service so the concept of a Voluntary Action Center means both of those limitations have to go.

Among the 70 fully operating Voluntary Action Centers across the country with full time staff, 206 in various developmental stages, we find all kinds of vestigial forms, as well as some very creative and innovative programs. In Albany, the State University students decided to start a Voluntary Action Center, instead of violence, after Kent State. The student movement has injected all sorts of responsiveness into the concept. No longer are we saying this is an employment agency for volunteers to serve in existing agencies under supervision. We are saying VAC is much greater than this. Any agency has certain ground rules which volunteers must observe just as staff does. It's up to the agency to interpret the need for those ground rules. As an old caseworker, I question those about confidentiality: whom are we protecting? Often not the client at all! Certainly in the mental health field the patients say, "I'd much rather have you tell somebody in my home town that I'm coming home than not. Because then somebody will be alerted to help me when I get there." But for years we had a confidentiality block. You couldn't tell about people in a state hospital. The volunteer's freedom of action is important to *team* work with professional staff. The first step in forming a Voluntary Action Center, as in Binghamton, is an intensive study of agency needs for volunteers, not to go to an agency and say, "You should have a volunteer program—now how many do you want?" Rather, "What are the things that are not being done for your clients that you know ought to be done? Client needs that you don't have enough staff for, time, or enough allowed in the budget?" Volunteers can scrounge! They can mobilize resources to meet a specific need in ways that we can never do if we are on the payroll. We would jeopardize perhaps the large donation of a community resource if we ask for a special donation, but a volunteer can ask his neighbor on an informal basis which would not jeopardize his other contributions.

There has been a real revolution about the kinds of persons who volunteer. Industry is interested in volunteering just as individuals are. The traditional Helen Hokenson type is a disappearing species in our society. The higher a woman's education, the more likely she is to be found in the labor market. The woman who used to be the traditional volunteer is now active in a job, and statistically makes up a very small proportion of the population. Students didn't used to volunteer. I can remember when one of my daughters in college in the 50's tried to volunteer, she was hooted right out of her house. However, her younger brother, through with college last June, was educated as a volunteer. The life style of students has changed and they are using volunteering for career exploration. Their counselors are counseling them into volunteering, "Go watch a psychologist at work. Don't make up your mind that you are going to be a psychologist until you see what the job is like by working with one as a volunteer," for example. The woman who returns to the labor market also uses volunteering as career exploration, a way to test herself. Can she really work, can she really get dinner on the table if she is gone a lot? It's safer to test herself as a volunteer. Never forget this part of the motivation of the volunteer, or that a lot of people are dissatisfied with their work, and volunteer for a sense of accomplishment.

The National Center is going to have a mass media recruitment campaign. Your agencies will have applicants who are stimulated by television public service announcements which say "we need you." What are you doing about your community? If you want to help in your community, call such and such a number. Where there are Voluntary Action Centers that number will be inserted by the local station. Test runs have turned up some unemployed persons as volunteers, but young, employed men from 20–30 are the most frequent responders. Such persons want to work after five and weekends, and you can hardly get staff to do that. There is a function and a need for services at those hours, but we have to stagger staff so there is someone for volunteers to check in with when they are giving their time at non-business hours. In volunteering I changed my professional identity: I retired as a caseworker and the Girl Scouts made an adult educator out of me. Volunteer work as trainer stimulated me to go back for a degree in adult education because I had become so fascinated with the process of human development among adults. Volunteers can explore a new discipline, and change their identity. I had a very reassuring thought the other day, that unless you have periodic identity crises, you are not *alive*!

We have to provide access to citizens who want to do something about the very problems of our society through the Voluntary Action Center. Richard Cornuelle, in *Reclaiming the American Dream*, says it's the nature of human beings to desire to help one another. He is writing a new book now explaining that basic difficulty in our society today is the nature of our planning process, a very poor system for deciding who should do what, who should serve whom and who should pay for it. Wider participation in the planning process is important to the field of volunteering because the volunteer has a uniquely neutral stance in the program development process, neither consumer nor provider of service. He is an observer of service from a humane standpoint, not technical, analyzing the impact of services on persons, inconvenience of delivery patterns, etc. Councils of social agencies and agencies within them plan social service delivery systems.

What VACs can do is plan *receiving systems*, so that the people who need services know about them and can get to where they are offered. VACs will mediate with the agencies to be sure that they offer services where and when they will be used. An example from Planned Parenthood: one board had a very tempting offer from a medical college, while it was also struggling for money. The medical college said doctors in training now should have family planning experience so you can close up shop in your downtown offices and we will give you office space and free doctors and free nurses and free clerical services at our building. You won't have to do anything except meet as a board once in a while and review the program. Well fortunately some volunteers on that board had worked in direct services. They said, "If we move up in the college building, we will not be serving where we are most needed. Nobody will come up there." And so, what we did was to tell them, "Your doctors have got to learn how to work downtown. You come on down and participate in our facilities. You can help us open a couple of satellites but you are not going to lure us up on the hill where we won't be used." I think this was a good educative experience for the curriculum planners at the medical school as well as for us on the board of Planned Parenthood.

It's this kind of perspective that I think the volunteer offers in planning, goal setting and delivery system planning process. If you are a potential recipient or a parent of someone in need or have a personal stake in a service, this comes through and you are seen as pleading from a special interest need. If you are frankly a consumer, you are probably perceived as an adversary. We need a voluntary action center as an intercessor between the consumers and the providers to interpret both ways. A structure, I hope as flexible and informal as possible, is a means of communicating in both directions. I think that volunteers see the impact of services on persons not as clients, not as inmates, not as patients, but as *people*. Need for this is reflected in comprehensive health planning legislation where 51% of the comprehensive health planning group must be laymen instead of providers doing our comprehensive health planning. The watch-dog function of the volunteer without self-interest is terribly important. Where agencies really need help to meet real needs, this is where the volunteer efforts and priorities will go.

You will have some agencies that will say we can't get volunteers any more because women are going back to work. You will have others that have waiting lists of volunteers. It's not the nature of the tasks we give the volunteers, but whether they perceive that their service is really essential to solving problems. In health care, in 1970, there were 13 other countries that had a lower infant mortality rate than the U.S. According to World Health Organization, we are now the 27th country in female life expectancy and USA ranks 31st in the world for male life expectancy. There are 30 other countries which are safer, statistically, for men to live in. Yet we have very capable, talented and wealthy volunteers who are running gift shops and pushing flower carts in hospitals. There are people who could see the need, who could advocate the better distribution of medical services, who could do something about it, if they only realized the power they have.

We are hoping that a voluntary action center will serve as a convener for people who are heads of agencies, for people who direct volunteer programs in agencies, for volunteers themselves in certain areas, as youth serving as volunteers. All the youth group leaders in town could get a shot in the arm about the importance of their work with a film and discussion about youth programming. There can be cooperative training, there can be recognition of a very meaningful sort of volunteers. The national volunteer recognition program has been given to NCVA by Lane Bryant: two awards each year, for group and single volunteers. The nomination means a lot to people, knowing that outside of their community somebody else recognizes what they did was important.

Volunteering is good for the person who is volunteering. Preventing senility among senior citizen volunteers is why we have the Retired Senior Volunteer Program, as Title VI of the Older Americans Act. Your county should have a project. It will require a sponsorship by an agency, or a voluntary action center to cut across all agencies. The man who accepted the NCVA award last year for his S.E.R.V.E. group testified before the joint congressional hearing on the needs of older Americans. He told Congress his arthritis doesn't hurt on Mondays and Thursdays, the days that he volunteers. When youngsters in training schools serve as tutors for younger children, they have a great personality change because suddenly they feel a different self concept. They are important to somebody else and they discover their own strength through volunteering. The N.O.W. stance against service volunteering as exploiting women ignores the way many women have really found themselves through volunteering, and discovered abilities they didn't know they had.

I agree with Richard Cornuelle about a weakness in our decision-making process, that we need access for citizens to participate in the decision-making process. When they do it from a volunteer stance, they have an authencity, very important in overall planning, because otherwise we tend to do what we can do or like to do. While I was a caseworker, I thought social workers were going to reform the world. As I took up adult education, I thought that that was the answer. I still think there is great strength in both of those disciplines but I am trying now to develop another discipline in my new job: to develop education opportunities for the leadership of local voluntary action centers. I think we have a new profession emerging, out of about 30 disciplines in the field.

I brought along some special things about social services and volunteers in social services because I think these documents are very useful for other agencies too. This is for the local commissioner, when you get your new one: *You and your Volunteers, a partnership that works* because it is important in any agency to have executive endorsement, demonstrating by his behavior that the reward system of that agency is tied to a positive plan for volunteers; that he is not threatened by citizen participation and he does not want the staff to feel threatened; that he feels volunteers strengthen agency services. We have to *start* with him! Many services use friendly visitors in one form or another, this *Guide for Friendly Visitors* was written by a neighbor of yours in Syracuse, Ruth Sherwood of the Voluntary Action Center. It is supported 1/3 by Onondaga County, 1/3 by Onondaga United Fund and 1/3 by its own services. For example, pre-retirement training in industries is a course for potential retirees about volunteering as an activity after retirement, to start now as aid in the transition. Future Shock recommends one foot in the future and one in the past, to move back and forth. That's not the best model for you in a rural county. The Ontario County VAC would be a good one, because it started on a shoestring program, sponsored by a church, and began three years ago on a part-time basis. One of the things their executive does is very important. There isn't a meeting around about volunteerism which she doesn't attend. She says she needs all of the inspiration and new ideas that she can get, and so she talks volunteerism with everybody.

We all know that we don't learn only from experienced people in the field, we learn from the fresh view-point of new people, who are experimenting with what volunteers can do. The National Center has a "laundry list" called *Everyone Can Help Someone*, and that's my conviction. Not every agency can use every volunteer. We are saying there is a spot for any human being who wants to help another and we have to find the right spots. These examples were compiled from the program samples that came into the National Center's Clearinghouse. You might take it to a commissioner to show what volunteers can do to strengthen and reinforce professional services and expand them, really outreach. The National Center also produces a newsletter every month. This one happens to be on the environment and what volunteers can do on ecology projects, others on subjects such as school volunteers. There were so many ideas that came in on volunteers with youth that HEW has brought out *Volunteers Help Youth*, written by the Clearinghouse staff about the various fields such as probation, corrections, youth groups, education, tutoring, vocational counseling, work programs, etc. in which volunteers work with the young. Another book could be done on what youth can *do* as volunteers because they can do fantastic things. They haven't lived long enough to know you can't do something so they just go right ahead and do it!

In order to have a Voluntary Center, you really need an organization that would begin with a steering committee and emerge into an advisory committee if you decide to attach it to an existing agency or board of directors; you may want to incorporate by yourselves. Your steering committee would need two or three task forces, one to discover where volunteers are needed in the county, by working with the practicing human service personnel; with teachers, ask what help could you use in the classroom or in home visiting? Teachers don't have time to make home visits, but volunteers can. In child welfare, finding foster homes; in mental hygiene, bringing patients back into the community from residential care. The examples are as many as there are persons. The second would discover what are the *sources* for volunteers: Church Women United, the National Council of Jewish Women, the National Council of Catholic Women, the National Council of Negro Women, all are committed to volunteering as part of their function; as the Junior League. Youth groups look for service projects. We have seen some strange and wonderful appropriations of membership monies made by youth groups at the end of the program year. What they need is help to understand what the needs in the community are, what they can do to funnel those resources into spots where they are most needed. Industry gives released time for volunteering. Hour for hour. In Newark, New Jersey, three hours a week given of your own time is matched by three hours of the Prudential Life Insurance Company. This is not just for the President to sit on the hospital board, but it is for his secretary if she wants to take a Brownie troop on a trip. It is for every employee up to six hours a week. Zerox employees write up a proposal and then it is screened by a committee of their peers; this year they have ten full time employees doing a community volunteer project, some in agencies and some on their own. They are going to do this every year. It's getting to be the in thing in industry to have employees volunteering. On Manhattan Island there is an association with 38 members, everyone of whom is paid full time to find volunteer jobs for the employees of that company. In a rural county you are not going to find much of this, but you do have some in Norwich.

There is a real potential in Service Clubs. The Kiwanis committed its national membership to help with the development of a Voluntary Action Center. So don't fail to talk to your local Kiwanis members. What are they going to do? The JCs have a similar commitment in their "Do Something" campaign. VACs should connect local clubs with the needs. As you think about what could happen here, I hope you will bear in mind that you ought to have some of the clients of your agencies in on the planning as well as staff members of agencies. This perspective is important in the development of a voluntary action center. My favorite example is having been just a few minutes out of the recovery room in my local hospital when a lady volunteer insisted that I needed a book. That could happen without staff leadership, if you just bring in volunteers and give them a menial job without training. Volunteers need to understand what you are trying to do. For effective partnership, you have to develop ways for volunteers to work right along with staff, trying to accomplish the same things as the staff is trying to accomplish. Without training, volunteers are not going to stay very long.

We find that people are hungry for volunteer assignments. After a television series on conditions in state schools, the one that was cited, had 1,600 telephone calls in the next two days from people wanting to come and help, saying they would do anything. I think this is very significant. Lots of us would like to do something, we just don't know where to take hold. The voluntary action center should help people find their spot to help. We don't have any rigid patterns for these organizations. You have to tailor it to your resources.

Question: You spoke of three task forces and one of these task forces was to find where volunteers are needed and one was a task force to find where volunteers are available and what was the third one?

Answer: Who is going to pay for it. Where is the support coming from? Don't limit it to any single source. We did a survey of the VACs that existed. I think there were some 50 when they did the survey and they found multiple sources of support. Some churches have made this an overall church project, non-denominational, a complete community service thing. Chambers of Commerce are footing the bills. Cooperative Extension Staff are the key people in many of the groups in New York State. This doesn't mean financial support from Cooperative Extension, but leadership in the community to catalyze the resources that are there. Something like 16 different categories of sponsorship work with VACs. Most in the urban areas are part of the council or social planning group. A lot of VACs prefer to be independent, they don't want to be social service oriented, but *human* service, and want to be in education, welfare and health as well.

Question: What are some of the potential conflicts and problems over the emergence of yet another agency in a county or city situation? Particularly one that is playing the role that you have outlined as standing between. I think maybe one might use the work advocate of consumers or of the needs. I could see this causing some problems.

Answer: I think it would solve some too. Any coordinating agency is created because of duplication, gaps and the need to have one focal point in a community. A lot of the councils of community services are loosing some community support, and turning to the Voluntary Action Center as a relevant link for consumers to the council. We discovered the value of volunteer mobility. Every nominating committee choosing new board members is casting around for people who know what they are trying to do. The development process to give citizens sophistication, about community needs and the community planning process, is terribly important. There are problems with volunteers. You can get wacky volunteers just as you can get a wacky staff member. People need the benefit of careful orientation and continuous education. If you don't feel a need for a voluntary action center, you don't need to have one. I think you have to need it in order to justify having it. I believe we need them. Canandaigua had a total income of $11,000 in their first three years, started on a part-time basis with donated rent and not counting any in-kind. You know what your services are in this county. Salaries are pretty low in some areas as for attracting a competent staff, but on the other hand, maybe you need somebody from town who really knows the town, for whom it might be a second income. You need to build a budget, not only a salary. Some get started with volunteer help. We are talking about the sheltered workshop here in town. That's the way that started. A lot of things do start with volunteers but for continuity and commitment, I think you have to have somebody there consistently.

Question: You have not mentioned the small funds that the National Center did have. I don't want to put you on the spot.

Answer: We did have some money that has all been distributed. This was appropriated unexpended funds from three federal departments. Secretary Romney as chairman of the President's committee on volunteerism had seven cabinet members on his committee. They all looked at heir funds, talked to their comptrollers and three of them came up with some money to start voluntary action centers or innovative approaches in existing ones. Those monies came from HUD, HEW, and OEO. Once funds are appropriated for a purpose, that department has criteria to be applied in sifting of the projects: 32 out of 155 were funded. There may be other funding, such as RSVP, through ACTION. Through the state offices of aging, there are 15 million dollars being distributed across the country for senior citizen projects. The law enforcement aid program seems to have money. Many local courts are getting LEAA funding for volunteer programs in probation. In New York State the law for appointing powers for probation officers states the qualifications required and incidentally says that some of these people would be paid and some of them would not. Both will have the same legal prerogative and authority whether they are paid or not, so they can do the same things. In RSVP volunteers get expense money, in Foster Grandparents they are paid for actual service at minimum levels, not equivalent to the value received. You don't find anything about compensation in the dictionary in the definition of volunteer, but emphasis on freedom of choice.

Question: Who is liable if a volunteer is injured while working for you?

Answer: You aren't any more liable than you are for an employee. Most agencies have coverage for employees but a rider can be attached to those policies, agency by agency. We are actually negotiating in this and there has been a lot of research done. There are hundreds of insurance companies that write different kinds of coverage which have implications for volunteerism. The state department of mental hygiene has coverage for personal liability. The Attorney General ruled that volunteers are unpaid employees. Now the state department of social services has been working on this and some of the counties have their own for their volunteer program.

Question: Agencies may take insurance on volunteers?

Answer: Yes, individually or through other agencies. This is usually secondary automobile coverage, which means that if you exhaust your own insurance, this insurance comes into force to cover the supplemental obligation.

The consultant in the state department of social services says they now have it available. The local districts can ask through their regional office. People are slowly waking up to what the Harris Social Security Amendments in 1967 say. Hinged to Federal reimbursements there have to be volunteers and work opportunities for clients in every district. If HEW ever lowers the boom and enforces those 1967 amendments we are going to have a lot of counties wake up suddenly to the fact they are not going to get that 75% that is so crucial to them: not eligible because they have not met the requirements for volunteers and clients work opportunities. It says "paid volunteers". What it means is out of pocket expenses like the RSVP legislation promises in Title VI Older Americans Act. Enabling funding, I call it, or administrative support, is for out of pocket expense to the volunteer so that he can serve and not a salary or payment for services rendered.

10

Aspects of Volunteer Training

No one will be "trained" for long any more . . . Change is so rapid and full of ambiguities that everyone needs constant retooling and renewal of commitment to give confidence for action, and competence for leadership responsibilities. One change effected creates the need for many more.

Volunteers and staff alike seek additional education which will widen horizons of awareness . . . sharpen skills . . . deepen knowledge . . . heighten sensitivity to varying perspectives . . . apply insights from new discoveries. Educators must weigh the value of their intervention to create change.

Such learning involves testing assumptions which may no longer be valid, unlearning anachronisms . . . changing attitudes . . . some pain . . . some hard work . . . some time to take stock, to set new personal objectives.

In a climate which is supportive and appreciative of the meaning of the adult learning process, learning can be an enjoyable, satisfying experience, one which develops the person and his ability to solve problems and develops more effective patterns of collaborative effort. A training situation is a safer place to try new skills than the job situation. Many wise, warm people without teaching background can become effective trainers.

Training Today

The new thrust in volunteer training and education needs the

Presented in the VOLUNTARY ACTION NEWS Volume 3 Number 11 December 1972. A publication of the National Center for Voluntary Action, Washington, D. C.

perspective of potential learners in the early planning stages and the cooperation and advice of experts in the field of voluntarism. Volunteers who formerly served silently without contact with the program development process now must be brought into goal-setting, program design, service delivery and receiving systems.

Volunteers should be made aware of the significance of their perceptions of the impact of services on people, and speak up for those who cannot speak for themselves. This perspective will make training relevant.

There are immediate urgent needs and wider, longer-range issues which require research and development of theory and principles. Planners who set out to help meet emerging needs through training must consider:

   ...the volunteers to insure the best possible use of their valuable time and talents.

   ...the volunteer administrators with all the learning needs the emerging profession of volunteer administration requires.

   ...the paid staff working with volunteers on the job to develop understanding of the role of the volunteer.

   ...the public for their faith in and support of voluntarism.

Yet, there must be no illusion that training can be a panacea for all administrative and organizational problems which are inevitable in transition from earlier phases of voluntarism into the needs-centered voluntary action systems approach of today. At best—training provides an opportunity to test out assumptions and devise better roads to wisdom through the richer combinations of efforts.

NCVA's Thrust

Recognizing that volunteers and staff as well as consumers are entitled to reach for their own greatest potential levels, NCVA has established a new service—a Department for Education Development. The activities of this new department will be based on a series of surveys now underway:

   ...VAC representatives from the Regional Meetings rosters are being asked for opinions on priorities.

. . .educators are being consulted about new academic programs for staff and volunteers.

. . .voluntary organizations with long and wide experience in the training field are being asked to open their programs, and to combine forces on common interests.

. . .professional career membership associations are being asked for their opinions, favorite consultants, films, teaching aids and resource references.

In addition to setting NCVA priorities, the surveys will determine sites for demonstration and experimental training efforts.

Some training events will be operated by the National Center for Voluntary Action—particularly for local Voluntary Action Center staffs and boards. A series of workshops will provide the broad-gauged training our Voluntary Action Center people need to function effectively as community resource people. Specific subjects include administraton and management functions, community analysis, leadership and communication skills.

Selected, experienced Voluntary Action Center staff and volunteer will become part of a corps of trainer-consultants ready to teach at training events geared to Voluntary Action Centers, become faculty for college-operated courses or institutes, and share their experiences with agency people at the local level.

An advisory committee of knowledgeable persons and representatives from government, professional associations, the academic world and voluntary organizations will be organized. Some committee members will serve in the corps of trainer-consultants and help find and motivate capable people to join its ranks. In addition, the committee will assist in the coordination of educational efforts and advise on the development of curriculum materials and events.

Since the education needs are so great and the constituencies so diversified and spread geographically across the entire nation, NCVA will concentrate its initial efforts on stimulating a variety of training opportunities, college or community based, to give everyone some way to study not too far from home and with the least possible disruption of their job obligations.

The NCVA Clearinghouse will continue to store and disseminate information on study opportunities in the community and at colleges for volunteers and for staff. The *Voluntary Action News* will carry announcements of opportunities to study whenever enough lead time is given by the sponsors. Like other Clearinghouse information, it will be as valid and as timely as the contributions received.

Voluntary action demands high-level skills and courage to risk experimentation and new combinations of resources, highly focused on emerging needs. We ask you to help lessen these risks with your suggestions for training, good instructors, consultants for special subjects, good sites for short-term or academic study, etc. Particularly, we value word about opportunities in time to let them be known to the widest possible constituency well in advance of registration deadlines.

When volunteers begin working they neither want nor need the entire history of voluntarism, but they are eager for training in the ground rules for their first assignment. This is their "teachable moment."

Authentic information and practical experience acquired in training gives them confidence to take initiative rather than passively waiting to be directed. Adults bring life learned wisdom to training events, and test their experience for applying it in new roles, making training a mutual learning experience.

And training should nurture that original enthusiasm. Without it, the initial motivation to solve problems and effect change can quickly dissolve into frustration and indecisiveness. When unrealistic expectations are not met volunteers either give up entirely or, even worse, make others wish they had.

Above all, having a voice in planning his own training gives a highly motivated person a sharp focus and eagerness to learn. On the basis of his past experience, the volunteer is ready to learn what he thinks he needs to know to accomplish his tasks. He does not like to feel forced to re-invent the wheel, so training should offer visible help for immediate needs. It should begin where the learner *thinks* he is; only then will historical perspectives or philosophic abstractions seem important.

Volunteers are welcomed warmly, and feel welcome, when people see clearly what needs to be done and the ways to meet the goals. Training provides sharpened focus both for the volunteer and for paid staff.

This "bullseye" illustrates the fact that the learner is at the heart of all orientation and training. Orientation starts at the center of the bullseye with helping the individual test himself in a new situation and leads him out, step-by-step, through the wider concerns in a gradual learning process that culminates in his understanding of the benefit of his effort to the total community . . . and the value of tapping the community to benefit his effort. The cyclical nature of the learning process is represented by the smaller, continuously-moving, inner circle in the diagram. It indicates the new insights continually gained by the individual through ongoing interaction with all aspects of the orientation pattern, the new perspectives always returning to the center so that the individual learner can apply new meanings. The diagram illustrates, then, that training must educate both staff and volunteers in ways to face problems with mutual respect and trust . . . bringing out the fullest capacities of each . . . sometimes together around shared responsibilities . . . sometimes separately in specific job skills.

By supplementing basic knowledge with wider vision, new information and skills, training increases the volunteer's confidence and competence and leads him from his first, parochial anxiety, to wider interests and a forward look. It encourages self-direction and individual creativity and fosters the in-depth learning that follows naturally as problems demand new alternatives and fresh insight.

Training is for staff, too! Experienced *before* the arrival of the volunteer, training helps paid staff understand what volunteering means to people and how to keep the volunteers they have. Further, training helps staff and volunteers appreciate each other, gives them mutual confidence and respect and the ability to work together for common goals. The interaction tells the volunteer his accomplishments are valued and important. It makes him feel real progress, so often the crucial difference between dropping out and a deepening commitment.

Finally, and always, training should deal with ever-widening concerns, beginning with and returning in a continuous cycle to self-understanding.

Testing oneself against the requirements of each new situation means seeing what experience and skills are applicable and taking advantage of opportunities to learn whatever else is needed: about the work, about the clients, about the organizations, about the resources and changing needs of the community.

Training does not end with an introduction to a task, but continues until the task is finished.

Consultants Will Help

Nobody has all the answers for being a trainer, but utilizing consultants to plan training in conjunction with the trainees is a worthwhile effort.

Among the most helpful consultants:

• ex-clients and consumers of services—nobody knows what a problem means to people better than the person who has overcome it;

• experienced volunteers—often, volunteers articulate a human, non-technical perspective, neutral between the consumer and the providers of services;

- professionals, researchers with expertise and hobbyists—all contribute experience in the theory and technology of services;
- administrators—enthusiastic overseers contribute a strong sense of purpose, develop interdependence of staff and volunteers and ease communication and mutual trust;
- universities—schools of social work, adult education and urban affairs are anxious to prove and improve their relevance to today's community and people problems;
- cooperative extension and community colleges.

11

Executives Need Volunteers in Rehabilitation

Since other speakers have harked back to Moses, I would like to compare your role as Executive Directors to his in leading the Israelites toward the Promised Land. Jethro, his father-in-law gave Moses some very sage advice about delegating responsibility, warning him that he would wear himself out unless he involved other people in administering his leadership. A key person to whom you can delegate some of your responsibilities for community relations is the Director of Volunteer Services, and save yourself some wear and tear. Your agency needs to maintain good connections with your community, and this can take a great deal of your time away from other important functions. But as Jethro pointed out, you must choose able people of integrity, and place responsibilities on them.

Leadership of your volunteer program requires persons of professional level competencies, and you should select the one on your staff with great care. In delegating this responsibility you will demonstrate your backing for this person by giving him authority to carry out responsibilities which are of tremendous diversity and complexity. Most professionals deal with their clients in one-to-one relationships, whereas the Director of Volunteers is matching the resources of the community to the needs of your clients in a kaleidoscopic setting in which change is a constant factor and a way of life. He must be accountable to you for his trusteeship of the time and energies of many different persons, and of the resources they generate to enrich your program. He is accountable to your clients, for mustering appropriate resources quickly to meet their developmental needs

Presented at the Goodwill Industries Project May 23, 1973 Boston, Massachusetts.

as they emerge. A role implies expectations of other persons for appropriate behavior. You have a right to expect this head of department to report regularly his progress in enlisting community support. The clients have a respect for the Director of Volunteers as a sort of magician who can pull people out of a hat to do things they would like to have done. The community expects this person to respond to offers of help and gifts of resources quickly, too, since without quick acknowledgement the offers are seldom maintained for long: as the visible community contact person, the Director of Volunteers is perceived as the appropriate funnel into which the community pour its goodwill and interest to fill your program needs.

While the Director of Volunteer Services is channeling resources to the part of your rehabilitation facility which can make the best immediate use of help and materials, there are pressures from both sides of him: from the other staff members on one side and from the volunteers and community groups on the other. No wonder the Directors of Volunteer Services sometimes feel boxed into these four-sided pressures!

You at the executive level hold the key to his success. By your visible and tangible evidence of support, you can insure that he can keep his balance and not be thrown off by excessive demands from any of the other three sides of his square box:

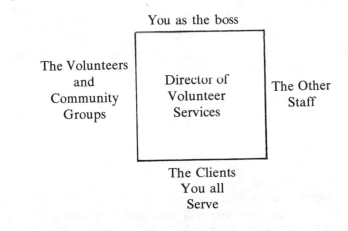

You as the boss

The Volunteers and Community Groups

Director of Volunteer Services

The Other Staff

The Clients You all Serve

Selection of a strong, yet flexible Director of Volunteer services is a very important decision. Take time to choose wisely, because this person can take a lot of pressure off you, if you back him up in his work. Make it clear that you have chosen carefully, and have faith in his ability to strengthen your program services. Look for a person of outstanding abilities—and judge personality characteristics just as important as, if not more so, than paper credentials. We are drawing such people from many disciplines now, and from the ranks of experienced volunteers. It is not fair, nor is it relevant, to hold out for academic degrees as the only index of ability, particularly since we have very few academic opportunities to prepare for this relatively new profession. It is an exciting time for those of us in the field trying to create a new profession, because our diversity is a great source of enrichment as we develop our own identity. Unfortunately, not all who have had educational advantages are groomed for success in this field. In low moments, I have sometimes felt that higher education has trained people to intellectualize so much they are paralysed into inaction with anticipated pitfalls, whereas the less sophisticated plunge ahead with a new idea and learn pragmatically from experience, often with great success at new approaches. Like the very young they don't know what "can't be done", and they go ahead and do it!

In looking for likely candidates, there are some personality characteristics which have proved very important for this work, and attitudes which indicate potential productive volunteer administration. Experience has taught us we need positive people, not skeptics. Negativism produces failure in a self-fulfilling prophecy sequence which is almost inevitable. Objectivity, yes, but not a cold analytical manner, but one of warmth. Honestly fair, he taking responsibility for his own feelings, so that he allows for his own loyalties and prejudices and compensates for them by giving other people the benefit of the doubt. Basic is a commitment to the preservation of the integrity and dignity of all persons, and a respect for their rights to develop to the fullest extent of their capacities. An openness to new ideas, and a seeking of new insights and learning are essential. No one has all the answers in this game, and you will need someone who is a real seeker after truth, not one who feels he has no more to learn.

Empathy, *accurate* empathy, as Charles Truax puts it, is essential. We need good listeners, who really try to understand how other people feel, and what is real to *them*, what they believe. We need people who accept the fact that man is really pretty irrational, and behaves according to what he believes, not the facts, lots of times. A warm acceptance as a person, leaving him feeling appreciated, goes far to releasing the fullest potential of a volunteer. And this means your Director of Volunteers has to be a good communicator, articulate in the written as well as the spoken word. The many people with whom he deals must really understand what he says, or he will be unable to carry the mediator roles between the consumer of services and the providers of services, between volunteers and staff who will work with or supervise volunteers. He must be teacher to both, and a motivator of both, to clarify their common goals and nurture teamwork in which each carries his own share of the work load. He cannot be autocratic and survive for long, he must be perceptive and sensitive to the feelings of all, and draw out their strengths and abilities, their life learned experience and wisdom to be applied to their joint efforts. He needs initiative and courage to take risks, and to learn from failures as well as successes. And we hope all of this is learned with a sense of humor—for then he can soar with the angels who can fly because they take themselves so lightly!

Obviously, you are going to have to settle for someone with human failings, somewhat lesser than this paragon I have described. But don't miss on too many of these qualities, because they are all important. Once you have chosen your Director, his success will depend a lot on you. You can make or break him in many ways—let's look at a few:

You must communicate your support for the volunteer program not by lip service and platitudes, but by demonstration in your own acts. Provide a convenient, accessible, pleasant office, with privacy for interviewing, a place to hang coats, to hold meetings, for records and storage of materials. The Volunteer Office and phone must be covered full-time, or the lack of response will dry up your resources. A good secretary and record keeper is essential as soon as your program grows beyond a few volunteers. Meals, out-of-pocket expenses and money for transportation and program supplies are important factors to get the people we need.

Your DVS should perform as head of a department, participating in decision making about program development and designing service delivery patterns. He'll have good ideas to contribute, but more importantly he has to know what's going on to make appropriate referrals. In your meetings you will communicate the value you place on volunteers, and staff will quickly sense whether rewards are going to the staff who extend and enrich their own work with volunteers, or to those who get rid of them as fast as they can. Give paid staff credit for doing more than they're paid for now—few people in rehabilitation are exceptions to this, and even they will try to live up to it if you assume they do. Help staff to see volunteers as available help for them to get things done they've been hoping to do but haven't had time or resources for. Encourage them to help recruit their friends as volunteers, to send them through the Volunteer Office to get a wide range of choice about where to serve. Help them feel free to invest time in orientation and training volunteers—it pays off in time the volunteers will give a hundred fold, if they have a good experience. Help them take the long view: time today, makes more time tomorrow for the important things they alone can do.

Share your community contacts with the Volunteer Office: your Director might be planning to approach the same people. Encourage staff to clear dates they know about and their community contacts so people won't be working in the community at cross purposes. Most of all, show your appreciation of volunteers by speaking briefly at their training courses and recognition events. A few words from you mean a great deal: that you care about volunteers and appreciate what they can do. Your being too busy tells another story, one which makes the job of the Director of Volunteers very much harder, and much less gratifying.

Encourage your Director of Volunteers to take training courses, attend conferences and community affairs. Like yours, his job has a lonely feeling: he's the only one of his kind on the staff, and he needs the reassurance and ideas he will gain from belonging to the professional organization of his own, the American Association of

Coordinators of Volunteer Services. Those forays into learning opportunities will strengthen your program and open up new resources. Pay his expenses, for you never will be able to pay a salary to cover all the overtime and personal commitment he brings to his job. You want him to keep up with current developments in his field, and there is no field which is opening up new potential any faster than volunteer administration. Help him to develop citizen leadership potential. You need informed, committed board members and fund raisers. The volunteers he can enable to progress to more responsible jobs will become a major source of community support for your programs and services. You need him, and he needs you. Together you can involve the whole community in meeting the needs of your citizens. Give him time to develop a good volunteer program, and you'll have time given to you in geometric proportions. Time is given to all men in equal amounts—more of it can go into your work, toward your goals, and without paychecks, if you appreciate the work of the Director of Volunteer Services. Give the volunteers the leadership they need, and the tools to work with, and you will be blessed as Moses was, with helpers to get *your* people into the Promised Land!

12

Motivation and Training of Staff and Volunteers

Motivation is as unique to individuals as fingerprints, but much more complicated. When volunteers are to learn, they are offering their time and talents, in fact, in many cases, really wanting to become involved enough for us to say they offer themselves. Then to choose to take training, is another freely chosen activity from which they may withdraw if they don't find what they want in the learning experience. Staff have livelihood at stake, and they have less freedom of choice, but they too know what they want to learn. The trainer, then, has to find out what people want to learn, and to help them to want to learn the skills and knowledge he knows they are going to need, which is not always what they think they want.

Thus, the learners must help in planning their training so they can come to understand what assumptions they have made which may not be true, and test their experience against what we know they will need to be able to do. This means there can be no one curriculum to fit all volunteers or all staff. Emphasis shifts and the learners have to take responsibility for teaching as well as for their own learning. We can't simply tell them what to do, we have to create a situation nearly like the real thing they will face, and let them discover how to apply their abilities in a new setting, and acquire some new ones.

Presented in the VIP Examiner, Winter 1973

Maslow has identified many human needs which are basic to all persons, starting with physical ones. Trainers have to assure comfort or learning can't take place. The learner must develop confidence and security if he is to learn appropriate behavior, and come to understand himself better before he attempts to influence others. This means that a climate has to be established in which it is safe to ask questions and admit what one doesn't know. People want to make friends and seem o.k. to their fellow learners, so trainers have to allow for sociability and free exchange of experiences before people are able to move toward meeting their higher needs for meaningful work and respect for their competence. They will really release their imagination and creativity if given a chance. This means the trainer will be learning a lot from the participants if he is open to new ideas, furture-oriented and not just teaching the ways "we used to do it."

In addition to these characteristics of all persons all the time, Eric Ericson has pointed out that as we grow, our needs change because our responsibilities and interests vary a lot according to our age.

Young adult people are highly motivated to meet people of the opposite sex, and to learn things they can use vocationally, even to deciding on a vocation. Older persons who are nearing retirement are looking for new roles, and the people in between are often feeling their work is dull and looking for more interesting and rewarding things to do as volunteers.

Another theory (Hertzberg) holds that energy levels are clearly tied to motivation. He feels that we are motivated by needs for belonging somewhere, for overcoming powerlessness and for achievement. The trainer may misinterpret apathy as lack of interest, whereas it really is confusion about what the things being taught are supposed to mean to the learner. He may not have had enough experience to realize what is important to him, so we have to give him some simulated experience to try first, and then he will form his own learning goals, which will give him energy to take training.

People all have different self-concepts, objectives and feelings because no one has exactly the same experience as anyone else. Everyone may have a different idea of "how it ought to be." We must deal with these differences and adapt our methods and content

to each person if we want him to learn, and try to find commonalities which we can build on in groups. If we don't, individual
learners will be thinking, "That's not for me," and be turned off.

The coordinator has responsibility for helping people visualize
the job requirements realistically. The administrator can motivate
people by lending his prestige to the training event, and interpreting his objectives, and his respect for volunteers. The client may well
be the one able to express what volunteers can do which is really
helpful, perhaps to show them what is real progress which they may
not have realized. The line staff are much more apt to want volunteers if they have had a hand in preparing them. Staff and volunteers trained together learn great respect for each other and can work
better in partnership afterwards. Ancillary staff need to be in on it,
too, or they will be unsympathetic to volunteers, even threatened,
feeling their jobs may be in jeopardy, unless they know the limits
of volunteer commitment and responsibility.

The best training develops an appetite for more. Learners should
continue to help plan what they want to learn because they have
learned what they need to know. Continuing learning is needed by
all persons at every age, and training can be the most exciting
kind, if it is relevant, active, varied in methods and fun.

13

Education for
Voluntary Action

In reviewing the current educational information available to the
voluntary sector, one hopes to stimulate more research and more
opportunities for learning. Since the purpose of this conference is
to identify the learning resources and knowledge requirements of
the voluntary sector, it should contribute ultimately to effectiveness
and efficiency of volunteers for attacking current national needs and
problems. From the perspective of educational development by the
National Center for Voluntary Action, high priority policy-relevant
needs-to-know center around local leadership: people who are administrators, both paid and volunteer. These persons influence
program goals and decisions, assess needs and evaluate programs
involving volunteers, and mobilize support for voluntary activities.

Leadership development programs are now based on obsolescing
experience and speculative forecasts.

The constituency of volunteers is no longer "housewife" dominated, but is enriched by high numbers of men, employed persons,
professionals in their livelihood activity, consumers of human services such as handicapped persons, the poor, minority groups, older
persons and other disadvantaged group members. Yet training lags
behind the administrative support for change.

Much written on the subject is based on untested assumptions
and generalizations. There are ambiguous values motivating both
volunteers and the emerging profession of volunteer administration.

Presented at the Conference on Education For Voluntary Action sponsored
by the National Center for Voluntary Action Washington D.C. October 1973

We have little accurate information on the number or nature of career opportunities for the burgeoning profession of volunteer administration. Inducing universities to incorporate curriculum for this vocation is difficult without explicit values and an accurate forecast of employment opportunities. Students are not being counselled into this field. We guess about where or how many positions exist now or are in staffing projections of voluntary and governmental organizations. Many persons carry some responsibility as part of other assignments under a variety of titles.

The capabilities of the facility or local organization staff director administering a volunteer program are crucial to the recruitment and retention of service volunteers and their progression into policy making and community planning positions. Both recognize their own learning needs *after* employment and cannot undertake long study away from a program without attrition of activities.

Regarding volunteer leadership, the transition is away from contributor or "name" boards toward broad representation. Working roles involve persons highly expert in fields of service, administrators, and consumers. Minority representation is no longer simple tokenism. Board meetings can be turbulent and drop-out rates seem to be rising. Both experienced traditional volunteers and the new representatives of minorities and needful groups in the constituency have to learn how to work together to improve their decision-making process, lest competing interests block action. Often the staff (serving ex-officio) are unable to mediate, or to make creative use of such conflict or assert effective leadership. We should identify the required skills and resources for learning how to attack community problems.

Volunteer administrators are under attack from Women's Lib for the low status of service volunteers. We have some evidence and need more about the value to volunteers themselves in service role experience: career exploration and rehabilitation are possible through self-testing and self-image improvement as well as altruistic gratification from being a giver as well as a receiver in service relationships. If this value could be documented, new opportunities could be opened for clients, patients, inmates and other persons unaccustomed to being considered volunteers. Volunteering should become a basic human right, not a privilege, as a learning method for citizenship development.

Welfare Rights Organizations and some labor union members perceive volunteers as a threat to paid jobs. Line staff in some organizations seem to feel this, too, whether or not it is a fact. The helping professions could be encouraged to develop operational definitions of their own competencies and complementary opportunities for laymen to reinforce their function and extend their influence. Each of the professions should define diagnostic and prescriptive functions for themselves so that volunteers might then motivate clients to use professional expertise effectively, and carry out recommendations during periods of practice and recovery from handicapping problems.

Volunteers have more time to listen than paid staff can usually spend. They can more readily exert more influence over community resources which could be brought to bear, enriching and humanizing services, beyond the budget and time limitations on staff. The "new career" and low status employee feels particularly vulnerable, and staffing patterns increasingly include all three, the professional, volunteer, and paid paraprofessional. We need research about how and where this is being worked out.

Budget pressures are building up with the termination of much federal category support. Competition for shared revenue is acute. Human services as intangibles compete with hardware interests, and usually do not come out with support.

The danger of volunteer exploitation is growing. The myth of free labor should be dispelled. Volunteers involve administrative costs, and the benefits accrued take time to be proved. Delinquency prevention, de-institutionalization and rehabilitation efforts can be amplified by volunteer participation, but we need proof that the long range benefits are worth the initial investment. Longitudinal studies could be implemented (with volunteer help!). The government needs documentation that current cuts will be expensive in the long run.

Human service cutbacks caused by federal policies related to categorical program support and income tax deductibility restrictions are demonstrably penny-wise and pound foolish, since more grave human needs are more expensive to meet. But we do not have actual facts to build this case.

Current policy decisions seem to be made by disbursing rather than service officials in both voluntary and governmental sectors. This could mean services are tailored to fit funding sources rather than needs requirements. Voluntarism will have to sharpen evaluation methods, and translate humane goals into quantitative concepts so that impact and effectiveness of services can be measured and reported understandably in cost/benefit terms. Unneeded services should be discontinued and needed ones justified so they will be supported. Volunteer advocacy is underutilized for interpreting current needs, and could be more effective in improving the human services with sound information based on first hand experience in a progression of developmental opportunities . . .

In the next three days as we listen and discuss the current perceptions of volunteerism we should bear in mind the following questions:

1. Can we get comprehensive information on the people now carrying paid volunteer administration responsibilities, titles, educational level and other qualifications, experience and felt learning needs?
2. Can we get more solid data from fields, with career opportunities, where positions now exist, or are projected? (The 1970 census figures, not yet released, will be limited to the "health industry" and clerical level positions then in existence.)
3. Can we maintain current information about where appropriate learning is being offered for vocational preparation?
4. The potential profession of volunteer administration requires characteristics which seem more important than credentials from educational experiences which were not designed with this vocation as an objective. To improve selection of candidates, can we develop tests for warmth, optimism, resilience, tolerance for ambiguity, energy, etc.? Can we suggest alternative sequences of educational experiences? Can we cross traditional departmental or discipline lines to make more effective combinations of current courses?
5. Can we survey the humanities for aspects relevant to develop a philosophical base and value system?
6. Can we survey the "helping professions" for identifying

complementary roles for volunteers, and their preparedness for supervisory and partnership roles?

7. Regarding volunteers themselves, is there any way to measure their numbers? Or the meaning of their experience, in terms of sequence leading to positions of power or influence on human services? Could there be contrasting parallel studies regarding the "new grass roots" volunteer with the "traditional" as to correlation of training with retention, diversity of interests with participation experience (for example: does the reality or potentiality of being a consumer qualify for or distort the participation patterns of citizens?)

8. What is the effect of their own experience as volunteers on clients? Mental patients, elderly persons, young predelinquents, welfare clients, civic groups allied in adhocracies around issues?

14

The Need for Education in Volunteerism

Americans have a tendency to depend upon individual charisma and initiative for solutions to community problems. Some of the cynics say "Let George do it." But most of us hope a prophet will point the way, and then we are willing to pitch in and do our part to get the job done. Too long serene in faith that appropriate able leadership always spontaneously springs up to solve new problems, we are now nearing a paralysing low morale of cynicism or panic as we recognize through modern media the human limitations of current individual leaders. It seems they don't understand the problems, or their focus seems limited to special interests. Some have a fanatic singleness of purpose on behalf of one constituency which threatens the general welfare. Myths of infallibility no longer reassure us. We must save ourselves.

One brighter spot on the scene is the growth of volunteering which demonstrates the positive side of the nature of ordinary men and women. There is a lot of real concern and desire to help, especially for the victim of catastrophe, illness, old age, economic disaster, or the accident of a disadvantaged birth. People *do* want to help people. They do want their help to count, to make a significant difference. In our segmented and stratified society, it is hard for helpers to reach those who most need help unless the problems have reached crisis proportions. Volunteers would like to *prevent* crisis, and to help not only during crisis but afterward, in the less dramatic but most important steps in overcoming damage or disadvantage through rehabilitation.

Trained professional help, and the money to pay for it, always seem to be in short supply. Inflation and recession compound the shortages. Volunteer person power is ready and willing, but not always *able*. Education and training are needed not only for the volunteers themselves but for the trained paid helpers on how to plug in the effort, skills and time which volunteers offer. A special function, volunteer administration, is a new career option attracting altruistic, able people who need professional level education to perfect a philosophy, a body of knowledge and discipline to apply skills effectively and ethically.

> "Intelligence is not something possessed once and for all. It is in a constant process of forming, and its retention requires constant alertness in observing consequences—an open-minded will to learn, and courage in readjustment."
>
> —John Dewey

Most people in leadership for volunteerism must meet John Dewey's standard for intelligence, or they do not long survive in leadership roles at the forefront of social change. Constantly confronted with crisis about support, they also face consumer demands for immediately responsive human services in ever new combinations of resources and delivery patterns. No field of human activity changes more rapidly in dynamic response to economic turns, new legislation or technological discoveries.

Volunteers, whom I define as givers of unpaid service who may need some enabling funding in order to serve, deserve a wide range of choice about where and how. Most are seeking to improve their own and others' lives, quick to react to new interests, they can experiment and move about with far less risk than established agencies or professional disciplines can. People elected to unpaid leadership of boards or committees are under tremendous pressures to keep their organization au courant with new trends. Other leaders, paid and appointed as Directors of Volunteer Services, suffer the same pressures even more intensely, and they have a career at stake, as well, to heighten their anxiety.

Both paid and unpaid leaders are begging for learning opportunities at the top of every list of needs for help, on all the surveys we see. People are traveling thousands of miles to events of good reputation, often at their own personal expense, and almost any event which is well publicized is well subscribed. There is no question about the need and the desire for more and better training across the country: several studies have come up with parallel findings. There is question about the quality, and faddism which distorts much effort. Not all events justify enthusiasm, although simply the opportunity to get together, to share common worries and reduce the ineffable sense of loneliness people feel in most volunteer administration career positions makes the sacrifice worthwhile.

Many short term non-accredited events suffer from what some of us as educators have identified as the Goldilocks-Three Bears syndrome: the bed of knowledge offered is too hard for some, too soft for others, and only a part of any event is "just right" for any one person.

Another phenomenon observed over a long period in volunteerism across the U.S.A. is the emergence of a few chronic students who attend everything possible, not always to observe consequences or readjust their practice to new concepts, but sometimes simply to renew friendships and to be identified with the small experienced "in" group who get around to the more significant regional and national opportunities. Adult educators have demonstrated that the more education persons have, the more they seek. For these people, the current, chaotic, uneven supply of learning opportunities may be minimally adequate. But educational needs for voluteerism are much broader than theirs.

Among learning needs which must be addressed is the much more widely felt sense of inadequcy to solve current social problems. New program, grass roots and academic realists brush aside sentimentality about volunteering being virtuous and fine, and seek to grapple with the tough realities of our depressed society. Many are dubious about the capacity of government adequately to cope with people's needs and the abilities of people to cope with government. The relatively recent national government sponsorship of volunteering is also viewed with some skepticism as national efforts prove much more expensive then local ones, and not that much more effective in fighting poverty, drug abuse, family disintegration and other chronic problems like juvenile delinquency. The urgency of government and people problem solving capabilities grows with every new issue. Revenue-sharing and the rest of the new federalism are forcing states and local general purpose governments to use national monies to solve local problems. Like a poorly administered volunteer program, in which volunteers are mobilized before their functions are defined, local revenue-sharing has dispersed to more than 37,000 units of government vast sums of federal tax revenues with very little help about how to use it effectively or meet accountability expectations. The most ubiquitous learning need in the U.S.A. today is for citizens to understand their own community needs, how to prioritize and plan to meet the most important and urgent ones, and monitor the process to hold the "experts" accountable for solutions.

Why is only a fourth of our population involved in volunteering? Because citizenship education has ignored the subject. The potential of volunteerism in our pluralistic, democratic, dynamic society is simply not being realized. Recent legislation and popularization has opened volunteering to new constituencies of volunteers. Two studies done nine years apart by the U.S. Census Bureau show a growth from 21.7 million volunteers in 1965 to over 37 million, only 59% of whom are women, in 1974. Old learning designs are totally inadequate for the volunteers themselves and for the staff who work with them. Yet many so-called helping professions have preparatory educational programs which are still grinding out graduates to whom work supervising or in teamwork with volunteers comes as a rude surprise on their first jobs.

Most unprepared for these new needs of all the leadership people are those who organize voluntary helpers. The Director of Volunteers or of a voluntary recruitment center can no longer be passive, pleasant and a pink tea manager. It takes a great deal of knowledge about human growth and behavior, about human aspirations, about personnel administration with intangible (non-salary) reward systems, about orientation and training, about communication through groups, publications and the media, about managing an office, about accountability for work records, references, fiscal controls, and the cost/benefit relationship regarding contributed community effort and resources. One major function, counselling people, means that the needs of the client or consumer, those of the agency and of its staff must be matched to needs of volunteers themselves. Certain basics are essential in any field of volunteer placement. Much earlier training was concerned only with techniques. We have evolved a teachable technology, but we will have real professional level competence when we deal with the "whys" as well as the "how to's" in all our educational efforts.

A most striking example of the varieties of education required is drawn from the field of education which shows the complexities involved. Take a child with special learning needs in a short staffed school (and what school can truly individualize every study program without volunteers?) and as tutor a lonesome grandparent whose own family lives too far away. Here needs of the child, the teacher, the school and the volunteer are all being met in one mutually satisfying voluntary relationship.

In order to maintain such complex mutually satisfactory situations, the teacher needs learning in basic or continuing professional education about how to delegate manageable parts of the teaching process to volunteers: how to divide the work into feasible units for an amateur to handle; how to guide the tutor toward greater independence; how to nurture an affectionate relationship which can do so much to motivate and enhance the teaching-learning process.

The volunteer coordinator or director needs considerable learning about analysing people, identifying and matching the needs of clients (tutees) and teachers, to one tutor chosen from all the kinds of people who may think they want to be tutors, of whom not all would be appropriate.

Under 1974 Elementary and Secondary Education Act Appropriations, every beneficiary school is to have a Parent Advisory Committee. These members may not think of themselves as volunteers, but they probably will work with no compensation and use the resources of the Volunteer Director's office to accomplish their work. This new law suddenly requires a new set of duties and relationships within most of the elementary and secondary schools in the land. It is likely to increase pressures for individualized teaching and new curriculum experiences which will require volunteers in classrooms or other helping roles. Such is the relationship of volunteer administration to today's schools where two million volunteers were active in 1973.

One State Teacher's Union voted against having volunteers in local school systems, but not one local union in that state adopted the policy. The reason given was that no school system which had volunteers (for tutoring, classroom assistance or advisory committees, etc.) had failed to get its school bond issue passed—volunteers were worth the investment!

Teachers have come to value volunteers as advocates for educational goals more quickly than some other helping professions which still resist having volunteers. We should tell the teacher's story, to social workers, recreationists, speech therapists and other new disciplines which could use some salesmen for their function, too, as all community budgets get tighter. The professional education for each of these disciplines should prepare people for volunteering and working with volunteers.

The trend toward using volunteering to facilitate education has been rapid and venturesome, taking many forms. Seeing and even being volunteers is good for the students as part of their citizenship and humanistic development. Students serve within their own schools and in appropriate community programs. For them, such field experience volunteering is career exploration and a way to improve their feelings about themselves: anyone feels better when he knows he helped someone! Now older students with learning problems are teaching younger ones, and improving their own performance as much as that of the youngsters with whom they work. In a tight job market, paid work study opportunities are getting more scarce, but more volunteer opportunities are opening all the time. Field experience education through volunteering is enhancing the human service programs in communities just as work-study programs are benefiting unions and businesses. Both consider such arrangements effective upstream recuitment. Educational administrators need to see and to communicate the difference in philosophy and methodology with students in a classroom from helping them maximize learning in actual work situations, paid or unpaid. Agency staff training can be greatly enhanced by faculty knowledge of research and active participation, with actual application of theory to practice. Collaboration deepens the mutual understanding of faculties and practitioners of one another, and helps to build knowledge for both.

The linkage of researchers and practitioners is promoted through volunteerism in many fields of human services. Education has been used as an example because it is not only a field of activity replete with volunteering, but as a discipline it is in great need of observation and field-testing opportunities in order to keep up to date with societal needs and evolving solutions.

Educators in their search for relevance to meet current criticism of their programs, urgently need citizen advocates who will develop conviction and commitment by participation with educators in the program planning process. This is an age of skepticism about experts and increasingly articulate consumer dissatisfaction with government services or those of voluntary agencies in proportion to their costs. More citizen participation in goal setting and planning is essential to build community support for needed services and keep them focussed on their basic purposes. All agencies have a tremendous public education job to do, and cannot do it alone or through public relations methods. More citizens need to be *active* in programs in order to take up the cause.

Some organizations have lost sight of their original purposes in their struggle to survive because not enough volunteers knew what they were trying to do. Their structures became ends instead of means toward altruistic ends. DuChardin has said "Tender beginnings are lost in the woody growth which follows." Human organizations need constant new blood and fresh perspectives to keep them flexible and responsive to changing needs. Board and committee training must preserve the spontaneity, the altruism, the humane, non-technical approach which will preserve the tenderness of original purpose and prevent the rigidity, "woody growth". To retain credibility, management training must stress accountability.

A learner for voluntarism is doubly a volunteer, for the education as well as for the work that is undertaken voluntarily. To maintain and build interest and commitment, the learner must be deeply involved in planning his learning and maintaining a searching, seeking climate for everyone involved. There are reliable cookbooks or road maps for the simple techniques of recruiting, finance accountability, etc. There are experienced experts to teach in these areas. Learning *leadership* is sorely needed however, which can stimulate and nurture originality and creative combinations of prior knowledge to be applied to new problems. The androgogy of Dr. Malcolm S. Knowles is far preferable to a pedagogical, authoritarian teaching style, but the competence and knowledge of the teacher and use of life learned wisdom among the students outweigh teaching gimmicks. We tread a fine line between totally process-centered teaching and task-oriented heavy technical instruction. Fads in methods come and go, and it is increasingly clear that we need a wide range of learning opportunities for all sorts of people. Schedules must accommodate personal obligations to families and to jobs. Costs must be kept reasonable and scholarship resources must be developed. Those most in need of learning opportunities may well be those least able to pay for them. Our geography is vast, and travel expensive. Learning opportunities must be created by the learners and the teaching resources most conveniently available, with advice from national experts. Continuing education has become a necessity for everyone who wants to survive in today's world, as volunteer, board member, volunteer director or just plain concerned citizen.

Volunteerism may be the last bastion of compassion in our society. To be really effective, it requires competencies and confidence in ordinary people to assume leadership and the grace to work collaboratively with all sorts of other leadership as well. It could well be that democracy depends on it.

Much thought about current problems is based on untested assumptions or obsolete facts. Education for volunteerism has to help people to think for themselves, to collaborate, share perspectives and build on common interests. Learning only happens in a climate in which it is safe to ask questions and give opinions—tomorrow's problems require a mind not only open to new ideas, but with the courage to readjust and apply them—as John Dewey reminded us!

15

The Consultant In Voluntary Action

Being asked to be a consultant is a heady experience, even remembering that an expert has been defined as a person fifty miles or more from home. In contrast to the role of a trainer or an executive with the power of authority and accountability in relationship to the people who are learning, the consultant is not a decision-maker for them, but an enabler and facilitator of their own decision-making. The National Center for Voluntary Action is launching a consultant network to offer skilled service to local programs on request, to minimize travel costs and multiply the potential for immediate help.

The group requesting a consultant has important preparation to do *before* he arrives on the scene. People with access to many others in the organization should have priority on his schedule so that their learning can benefit as many as possible. To use consultation effectively, they all need to assemble documentation for the data they will give him and focus their inquiries for a clear purpose. Group and individual conferences should have a logical sequence. There should be a planned use for the information shared. The schedule should be loose enough for flexibility, and organized on a priority basis. Otherwise, the time will be used less productively.

Sometimes one faction in an organization calls in a consultant to reinforce archaic patterns, or to serve vested interests. The consultant needs to look beyond what a few people want, to help the organization as a whole to understand what they really need, which may not be the same things. Consultation takes many forms: interviews, meetings and planning training, sometimes with the consultant in teaching roles at the training. Training is not a panacea for all the ills of organizations nor a means of controlling people, but should be a free learning opportunity to help people develop their potential abilities and learn to use them appropriately. Consultation must take a future oriented, problem solving approach like training, and neither process should be a backward look at "how I used to do it". A group requesting a consultant should involve him in deciding what form of help will be most productive. They may discover common learning needs among enough people to make training appropriate, and plan a training event to give those people the knowledge or skills which they seek, tapping many resources. The need for change must be validated so that the consultant is justified in exercizing his right to intervene, and will have support as he uses the appropriate methods. Records should be kept of the helping resources mentioned, and of the process experience for various parts of the organization. As goals are articulated, good insights should not get lost. They may be useful later, if not while the consultant is there. Some "throw away lines" contain real gems, never recovered after the enthusiasm of the moment has gone.

Consultant authority is based on expertise and identity as an outsider who has no vested interest in the outcome. Charles Hendry has identified three kinds of "headship":

The Head, who is employed or elected or assigned to give
    leadership.

A Head, whose personal characteristics of prestige, age, social
    status or charisma make him a leader no matter what his
    role is supposed to be in a given situation.

Ahead, the person who by greater knowledge and foresight has the
    authority of greater wisdom and greater influence because
    he "makes sense" to people.

The consultant must be *ahead* of the people he serves, in breadth of knowledge, in range of foresight and in powers of persuasion. He does not *tell* people what to do, but provides accurate help to facilitate their *own* decisions based on sound information and process. The functions he performs may be grouped in three partly overlapping categories: diagnostic, building trust, and communicating effectively. He must be clear about the differences between authority and power, and derive his own power from authenticity and competence. The decisive power rests with the people to whom he gives both information and confidence to make sound decisions. Participation in the consultative process should be broad, so that viewpoints of the management, the clientele, the line staff, administrative and service volunteers go into building real consensus on those decisions. Objectivity, fairness, warmth and concern as well as courage are essential characteristics for being a consultant. He needs individual and group counselling skills.

As a diagnostician, the consultant must take a reading from all of the constituent parts of the organization he serves. Facts include feelings as well as legal statements, such as constitution and by-laws. Individual self-concepts and the blocking and facilitating forces must be seen. Considering these factors, his weight is often used to achieve a better balance in an uneven distribution of power, in order to keep an organization and its constituency from being torn apart, or turning into non-productive paths. For example, a finance committee may be blocking program development. In order to facilitate achieving the purposes of an organization, the consultant must be aware of how weaknesses and strengths affect decisions and then emphasize information and helps which will strengthen leadership and give confidence to the people responsible for the future activities.

Clues lie in the experience of decision-making which the people involved have had and the tone or climate of the organization for sharing leadership. Where have the decisions been made? By the executive? In the Board? The *whole* Board? By the staff? By the funding sources? How ingrown and parochial is it? How open to new leadership, or sharing leadership at all? Have decisions made by a few been carried out by others? How's morale? Who is unhappy? Finding out why will give clues for corrective action to restore balance, and broaden participation. Sometimes responsibility is abdicated, creating a vacuum for role confusion to thrive in. Spotting the locus of authority saves a lot of time in identifying problems.

What are the communication means used—who hears what from whom? Openly, or not? Is the grapevine more active than formal patterns? What would strengthen communication so that the "in" group is broadened? Who is scapegoating? What provision is there for open discussion? What is the attitude toward candor and new ideas? Do rewards go to innovators or to people who don't rock the boat? Where do ideas come from? Where do people *believe* they come from? How consistent is the structure chart with the patterns for meetings as to participative decision-making? How congruent are individual goals and objectives with the purposes of the organization as a whole? Who is *"the* head", and who is *"a* head"? How far apart are they?

Such a reading is achieved only through mutually respectful relationships, and open opportunity for access to the consultant. He can do a great deal to create a climate in which it is safe to differ, to test assumptions, to introduce creative thinking. As an outsider, temporarily there, he can reinforce these positives with sensitivity and alertness. He can throw his weight where it is needed to strengthen the democratic process, encouraging the inarticulate, giving power to the powerless. Any group will have problems in these subjective areas. Democracy, as Edouard Lindeman said, is always in the process of becoming, never perfected. The consultant is far more responsible for the process than the product, in contrast to the evaluator. He can heed early warnings and mediate schisms. He can stretch horizons and point out resources. The accuracy with which he identifies the situational factors will determine his effectiveness. He draws out and encourages people, so that they can really understand what remedies or strategies might be helpful. Only if he is a good listener, and objective about what he hears, will his suggestions be useful.

While he is getting relevant information, the consultant is building the relationships, another determinant of how effective he can be. He must accept the right of persons to have opinions, and respond to them as persons whether he agrees with them or not. His receptivity becomes a model for others. His real success is measured by what they are able to do after he is gone, how they feel about it and about one another, what kind of access he has opened for them to have to one another.

What he says as an outsider may be similar to what some individuals there already have said, but he will be listened to as an expert. Because he comes in from the outside, the objectivity of the consultant is important in helping the people there see themselves and each other with new insights. The tone of his questions and comments can make this a very helpful experience for everyone. Sometimes a major contribution may be to help people delay what would have been an abortive decision, or one which some persons might make with internal reservations which would limit their enthusiasm in carrying out their part of the responsibility.

There are many ways to give suggestions and pontifical advice is seldom a good one. Exhortation leaves people feeling guilty and inadequate. The saddest words in the English language are "why didn't you?" Far more productive is "have you thought of—?" or "how would it be if you. . . .?" Then people can face forward with hope and specific expectations. Experts in motivation relate energy levels to clarity of goals. Congruity is crucial: clearly, overall goals must accommodate individual objectives for achievement, for power and for good relationships, in varying combinations. A consultant can help keep people from losing interest and keep organizations from faltering if he clarifies commonalities. He points out how overall goals could fulfill the wishes of individuals, who naturally wonder "what's in it for me?" Good goals are reasonable, flexible and can be measured. Sub-goals and objectives for certain activities or functions have to be compatible with the overall goals and the purposes of the organization, and meet the needs of the people who have to carry them out.

Brainstorming, with no judgmental comments to discourage creativity, has a high potential for producing good ideas. However, ultimately these ideas must be judged, prioritized and tested in discussion. Without the last step, people are confused by a welter of conflicting ideas and emotions which could paralyse future action. Ideas have to be evaluated, organized and projected by highlighting future implications in that judging process. Here is where the consultant's expertise comes in—that's why he was asked to come. He will have much more to work with if all the people have had a chance to throw out their ideas before he does. Together, they set the goals and imagine and test alternative strategies.

The process of consultation means thinking through with people all the information and perspectives thay can muster before they decide on and rank alternative strategies to carry out a purpose. Compromise leaves everyone feeling cheated. Consensus is a lot harder, but well worth the effort and time it takes, paying off in the effort and time people will give in purposeful work to be done afterward.

In testing alternatives, there are some frequent attitudes which surface because no one really likes to change, to give up cherished assumptions or to unlearn things which are no longer true. Someone almost always says:

—"We tried that once and it didn't work"

—"We are different here"

—"This is nothing new, we've heard it all before"

—"It won't work"

The consultant can make it safe and acceptable to doubt, to reveal ignorance, and to test new ideas. He can point out new factors which increase chances for success, within the organization and outside it. There are myths that inhibit honesty, and only with candor can we get at the truth, or examine a new idea. One example is the rampant myth that people who volunteer are so virtuous they ought to be free to do whatever they want. This makes it impossible to help them grow, or make certain that what they are doing is really the best thing they could do. There is great anxiety about rumors and many beliefs are not based on facts. Unfortunately, we act on beliefs, not facts. If a consultant is to do any good, he has to help dispel such beliefs and substitute the truth. Then people can decide what to do differently with all the information and resources they can muster. The more they discover in themselves and in their own setting, the more lasting will be the effect of the consultation.

The consultant then is a seeker of accurate information as well as one who shares his own. Quick ready answers cut off this process of self discovery and meaningful consideration of alternatives. The consultant reveals resources beyond the ken of the people he is working with. He may refer them to other lodes for information or potential help and technical assistance. Whatever he does had better be consistent with what he says, or he will lose his credibility. Being a consultant is a tempting role, but it carries with it some humbling responsibilities, as well as opportunities to learn a lot. His integrity and his competence are on the line. Often the relationships he builds become lasting friendships, and in voluntary action settings, this means developing the connective tissues of a movement. It is inspiring, if awesome, to realize that the good one can

do will live on. It is just as inspiring to a requesting group to make
optimum use of outside expertise and see beyond their own community and their habits the real potential for voluntary action to
improve the quality of life for us all.

16

Mobilizing the Efforts of Volunteers for a Just Society —are They Effective?

This complex title calls to mind some very vivid images. Looking toward the bicentennial, picture General Washington calling upon the concerned citizens of the colonies to fight for independence from an unjust ruler across the ocean. Think of John Gardner and the tremendous response to Common Cause in our own day. As a child, I saw in my mind's eye the familiar tricorned figure standing on a hill top, "calling up" the farmers and trades people, and lines of people converging up the hillside to find out what they were supposed to do. As a charter member of Common Cause, I have some of the same feeling: if I am being "mobilized" then tell me what I can do to get into the action. How do I become effective? Can I, as an individual, really make a difference? Where do I start? Who's going to lead me? Where do I get help to know what needs to be done? How can I know when I'm on the right track? When I have achieved something worthwhile?

As a member of Common Cause, I am deluged with tracts about issues. I am moved to write my legislators. And sometimes I wonder why, when I seldom get an answer. Sometimes things happen afterwards which tell me other people have written, too, and there are encouraging developments here and there which tell me it was worth the effort. I vote for officers whom I don't know, but I send

Presented at a National Conference on Social Welfare—May 22, 1974— Cincinnati, Ohio.

in my dues, feeling rather virtuous not to count them at income tax time. Sometimes Common Cause gets involved in issues which have little meaning for me, and that's when I don't do very much about them. So it goes with volunteers. What makes them effective?

Evaluation of voluntary action is a major concern to administrators, and to volunteers. Instead of evaluating people, methods are being devised to define desirable outcomes against which performance can be measured—not the person, but the impact on clients, organizations and the volunteers themselves of given services. Counting hours tells us little, but that is a truncated pattern habit which is hard to unlearn. Retention figures are far more significant, and the turnover of volunteers is not much different from the turnover of paid workers in the studies we know about. Far more significant are the instances of change in staff and client attitudes toward volunteers, the reversal of senescence in older persons, improved self-images of handicapped persons and juveniles, the women and college students who make career choices or create paid jobs for themselves based upon their volunteer experiences. As David Horton Smith, the Executive of the Association for Voluntary Action Scholars says, "One does not have to 'measure virtue' to do a good job of evaluation. . . . . but rather invest a small fraction of one's effort in self study in order to be able to improve one's effectiveness relative to inputs of time, energy, money and materials." The foundation of evaluation is the value system of the services, and the objective to improve them.

Our title for this session has key concepts: *mobilization, efforts* which are *effective,* and a *just* society. Realistically, we know that not all paid staff efforts are effective, and volunteers are human, too. Sometimes their efforts are effective, sometimes not. We all work together among forces which tend to measure effectiveness in the monetary terms of cost/benefit. The price must be right. But real values are intangibles: freedom, compassion, cooperation, respect for the integrity, dignity and right of each individual to develop to his or her greatest potential and economical use of resources—a just society. Only constant concern, vigilance, and concerted effort will guarantee intangible values and accountability for human resources. We all want to eliminate waste, more tragic when it's waste of people than of things.

Experience has proved certain factors are essential in mobilizing volunteer efforts and making them effective; which really means keeping volunteers long enough for them to focus their efforts toward shared objectives, and achieve desirable results. In logical sequence, these factors include:

1. An honest analysis of what needs to be done.
2. Target recruiting of the people to do the volunteer share.
3. Careful matching of assignments to interests and capabilities.
4. Monitoring for signs of discomfort and growth.
5. Providing for appropriate learning, mobility and recognition.

Managers of paid workers have found these factors important, but they can be compensated for deficiencies with a salary reward system, whereas volunteers must get their reward in other forms.

We must work out explicit objectives with volunteers emphasizing the special significance of their being volunteers, not paid for their service. Psychologists tell us that human energy depends on clarity of goals. Most of us, when we volunteer, have a sort of "rescue fantasy" not unlike the way each of Washington's recruits must have felt in response to his call: they were convinced that each had a necessary and important role in the great effort to achieve freedom. Volunteers are interested in why needs exist and what can be done to meet them. Most of the time Washington could persuade his volunteers to do what needed to be done, and his troops were fired with dedication and commitment to the cause. But even he had real trouble in springtime, when a soldier was likely to take off to get his spring planting done, or late summer, when the harvesting had to be done. American Revolution volunteers, like ours, had primary obligations which interrupted their service as volunteers. Historians have called them undependable. But they won the Revolution because it was possible to plan campaigns and peak work loads so people could meet their personal obligations as well as their volunteer obligations, and feel satisfaction in accomplishment of both.

Part of the morale problem in today's army is rooted in the fact that modern army life makes greater demands on persons to forego their primary obligations, and the cause of "defense" is so diffuse that individuals don't feel very important.

Be realistic about primary obligations. For volunteers, their volunteer work is seldom primary. People who find volunteers effective treat them with consideration and often evoke truly heroic service in today's revolutionary world. Feeling important with a sense of purpose is essential to volunteers. Clear goals, with belief that one is essential to the cause, unleash amazing energies. To tap this resource, agencies will have to have flexible service opportunities to accommodate people with full time jobs (who are the ones responding in significant proportions of the NCVA national ad campaign) and shifting life styles. Short term intensive assignments are attracting people of great ability to volunteering.

Those who haven't worked with volunteers believe that recruitment is a formidable first step. In training courses for new volunteer administrators, this anxiety is hard to allay. How-to's and "Where will we get the people?" are their first questions. But getting volunteers is not really a problem if there are important things to be done, and a good climate to do them in. Effective volunteer programs have waiting lists because people really want to be effective. A good climate includes all kinds of volunteers, particularly victims of a misfortune or problem, who understand better than anyone else how important it is to do something about it. Volunteering is no longer a privilege of already advantaged people, but a right which must be guaranteed imaginatively.

A good climate uses all sorts of talents, based on understanding that the urge to help is as natural as other more notorious and newsworthy human urges, for power, or sex, for example. Most people need to be needed. We humans have a great capacity, and a need to transcend our self-interest and give of ourselves. Maslow, in his late writings, began to interpret his concept of self-actualization in these terms. Self-transcendence is the ultimate development of self, which most of the world's religions have long recognized. Our whole society could be leavened by the kind of individuals who choose to realize their own fuller potential through getting involved in external goals. If we open more opportunities to volunteer, more persons will work to create a just society.

With the advent of the many national volunteer programs, such as the National Center for Voluntary Action and its Voluntary Action Centers, this natural human urge to help others has been given many channels for self development through improving human services as a volunteer. Voluntary action is not the old condescension of doing for others. *Action* is the significant word. We are saying not only that service roles are important, as indeed they are, but that the volunteer should be able to influence the planning process for developing new services, setting goals and priorities, designing new delivery patterns. Having participated in program development, the volunteer will go to bat for that program. Volunteers make the most authentic advocates for services because they seem to be speaking not for their own needs, or as part of a job, but on behalf of others without self-interest. This gives an authentic ring to what they say. There isn't a human service in the country which does not need this kind of advocacy at every level, from helping the recipient of a service understand how to use that service, to helping the Congress of the United States right injustices and persuading budget allocation decision-makers to assign resources to more humane priorities.

General Revenue Sharing is a case in point. The first year of experience in giving monies to local community decision-makers saw only 3% of those funds going into human services. Even the Treasury Department is concerned, and the Office of Revenue Sharing now has a phamphlet called "Get Involved" urging citizens to get into the allocation process, to make sure that new federalism resources are distributed more equitably, and local governments can respond to the most urgent community needs. Until recently citizens had recourse only through the ballot box after federal funds had been obligated, but the challenge now to those of us seeking a just society, whether we are paid or not, is to influence the decision-making process *before* funds are obligated. We must insure that worthwhile services both new and those formerly funded by federal categorical grants, are continued under Revenue Sharing. The new federalism has two prongs: cut backs in categories and local decision-making. The people least able to speak for themselves have been the first casualties: users of mental health centers, children, the disabled, the blind and the aged. Volunteers can articulate emerging needs not as consumers or providers of services—they are not at risk personally, and they have their own orbits in which to reach the seats of power.

Citizen action must make the difference. I doubt that the people in Pasadena felt that lights and paving for tennis courts was the most urgent problem they faced, yet nearly 1/2 million of revenue sharing funds went for that purpose. One rural county in Maryland still has its whole allotment in the bank, waiting to decide what to do with it. The monies go where people care enough to work to put them.

Here's where informed volunteer advocates come in: they perceive real needs from first hand observation. No longer do we just "use" volunteer services. That concept of volunteering is the kind of band-aiding and exploitation of good will which the National Organization of Women rightfully objects to. We have to offer volunteering which is action to improve the quality of life for the people with acute problems, and also for those who do something about those problems.

Effective volunteers take their cues from staff expertise, so staff partnership is crucial to their staying power. Recently recognized by the Department of Labor is an emerging profession of volunteer administration made up of people responsible for making volunteer efforts effective. Whether these leaders are paid or not, they see to it that volunteering really benefits the clients who use volunteer services, extends effectiveness for organizations and is good life experience for the people who volunteer. To break through the resistance of staff to using volunteers, they point out how volunteers can extend and reinforce staff work, and offer extra-budget services paid staff have neither resources nor time to do. They develop interesting, challenging roles for volunteers, who carry an important part in humanizing and individualizing services.

A good volunteer coordinator or director arranges orientation which leads the volunteer in, by showing how to apply good will and talents and valuable life experience. The coordinator will postpone the timing for a history of the organization! How many volunteers have been turned *off* because orientation began with ritualistic blessing of the founders! Orientation should turn people *on*, motivate them to achieve something better for their clients, and for their community. It should lead into continuous learning opportunities attuned to readiness. New volunteers also learn under supervision of experienced, able persons and in group training sessions where skills can be mastered and issues discussed in depth, taught by experts.

Most volunteers will tell you they got more out of volunteering than they put into it. Their freedom of choice means we must provide skilled counselling to find a good spot for each volunteer to start, and progressive growth opportunities to continue the challenge and deepen the commitment. Volunteers will be effective if their goals are clear, if they progress with both horizontal and vertical mobility, and they recognize the value of what they do because it is appreciated. Ivan Scheier, the great leader of volunteerism in the corrections field, says no staff member should do what a volunteer could do. We must analyse what needs to be done, find what volunteers could do and offer them the chance and help to do it. Whether these are service or social action opportunities is their choice. Their potential in the process for creating a just society is tremendous. Let's harness this volunteer power and see what human energies can do! There are great geographic injustices, as well as economic, social, racial ones in human services. Volunteers, as the connective tissue in our society, can do much to right these wrongs and to meet human needs. Each of us is a potential volunteer, and we all have work to do which could be much more effective and richer with volunteers around to help us and to lead us on to a better society. What are we waiting for? The Bicentennial should spur us on!

17

Volunteers are Worth the Effort

"In the mad pace and dehumanizing world we live in, volunteering is a way to improve the quality of one's life and that of others," states this authority. But she adds that organizations must provide staff support and orientation for volunteers so that their service is productive and personally satisfying.

"How do you do, Mrs. Smith . . . so nice to have you here today . . . it's just lovely that you want to help! Now if you'll just come over here . . . sit down at this corner of the table . . . we'll let you stamp these . . . and then you can put these in envelopes. After you finish those, you can address our magazine for physicians. Then we have lots of pamphlets to be counted.

Mrs. Smith smiles, but there is suddenly a seed of doubt in her mind. She got her house in order, shut the dog in for the day, spent her gas to travel 10 miles to the local voluntary association's office for *this*? Counting pamphlets may be somebody else's dish of tea, but it isn't hers.

In the mad pace and dehumanizing world we live in, volunteering is one meaningful way to make spare time count for something. It's a way to express concern and compassion for others, a way to improve the quality of one's own life as well as that of others. But most volunteers want to do something that fits

Presented in the American Lung Association Bulletin as a report from a Virginia Lung Association workshop.

their interests and experience. And, especially, volunteers must know what they are getting into and feel they have some say-so about what they are going to do. They don't want to be exploited.

It has changed

The changing pace of life has made it harder to find and cultivate those people who have experience, knowledge, skill, time, energy, and dedication enough to carry on the leadership function in our community agencies. These agencies therefore must place volunteers in attractive assignments, and provide the necessary training and staff support so volunteers get enough job satisfaction to sustain them.

Many businessmen who used to give their time now come home with briefcases of office work. Or they spend more time working on the house to cut expenses. Many women whose children are growing up or who have finished school now hold part-time or full-time jobs. And there's the phenomenon of volunteer fatigue. Numbers of people have not had good experiences as volunteers and are reluctant to try it again.

And the stereotype of the poor being legislated into positions of leadership is not providing an adequate answer, either. True, the concept of indigenous leadership promoted in the early 1960's has taken hold in many places. But it's still necessary to orient people of all backgrounds to the voluntary agency's goals. All persons need help to look wide and think big enough to decide agency policy, whether they perceive it as consumers or not.

Fortunately, young employed people, college students, and older persons are available for volunteer service. With considerate scheduling on the part of the agency, these people can make a tremendous contribution, counteracting the attrition among more traditional types of volunteers.

Development of leadership

Voluntary health agencies are a delicate mix of professional staff members and volunteers. In many agencies, the road to responsible leadership is a step-by-step process, beginning with direct service jobs. Volunteers then go on to assume a more and more powerful voice in policy-making.

People at the ALA tell me that many lung association volunteers start out on committees in areas of their particular interest and competence. Others start by assuming a special one-time job and move on to a commitment. One person has a friend with emphysema and joins a program committee to see that people with this condition receive comprehensive health services. Another person has had some experience in community air pollution control activities and wants to go on to more serious work in this field with the lung association. Still another is willing to work with school children in an imaginative antismoking program. Or whatever. The experience of seeing the program in action then makes the volunteers want to have a more powerful voice in policy making, and the committee service gives them the background for leadership as committee chairmen or board members.

Regardless of the specific roles that an agency sees for volunteers, it is of prime importance for the agency to make a real commitment to its volunteer program. The staff, the board, and the executive must be willing to give responsible administrative support to volunteers, and this means marking off a considerable amount of time for the work.

Each step of the way should be thought through before the volunteer is asked to assist. What work is to be done by the volunteer and why? What qualifications are important? Which staff member will stand by to advise and encourage each volunteer? Who will orient and train the volunteer?

Extension of the organization's arm

The keystone of voluntary activities is the concept of sharing work—of volunteer-staff teams carrying joint responsibility for tasks, projects, or continuing functions.

In organizations such as lung associations, which carry out programs that reach deep into the community, volunteers extend the work of the association in a way that could not be accomplished by the necessarily limited number of employed staff members. Volunteers, in their role with the association, provide skills and experience which would otherwise not be available to the organization.

Do you want your organization's ideas represented at public hearings on setting air pollution standards? You'd better get some real experts on your air conservation committee. Do you need a survey on community services for patients with chronic respiratory disease? There are lots of businessmen out there who know how to set up good surveys. Are you planning to contact corporations or foundations for funds for an important new project? Businessmen can help you with that. Are you beginning to explore the idea of getting a school established for one of the many new types of health workers now being developed? You'll need some educators, as well as medical people, for your initial committee work.

In these instances, the organization reaches out to the community for people with highly developed skills to assist with its programs.

Service-oriented volunteers who are willing to help carry out short-term projects also extend the arms of the organization. Do you need people to man an auto emissions check during Cleaner Air Week? Do you need people to staff an exhibit at a meeting of physicians or nurses? Are you planning to organize a health fair in the local shopping center? Do you need people to address those pamphlets? With staff coordination, orientation, and training, volunteers of many ages can take on all these jobs.

Every volunteer is an interpreter of your agency to his family, friends, and the other organizations to which he belongs. A corps of dedicated volunteers can do much to build community interest in and support for your organization. These ambassadors can mobilize resources, open doors, and recruit volunteers through all the other faces of their life. They come to the agency not from a vacuum, but from a network of connections with many other people whom the agency would like to reach with its message and services. But they will take a *good* message out into the community only if their volunteer experience has made them feel *good* about the agency. Staff members assigned to work with volunteers can do a great deal to guarantee the positives in that experience so that the volunteers feel appreciated, well placed, and productive as part of the agency.

We err in minimizing the need for orientation and training.

The truth will out, and the agency loses credibility when the volunteer gets the whole picture if we have not given him realistic expectations. Encourage experienced volunteers to take on new volunteers who can learn from them; nothing helps us think through what we do like having to teach someone else. Vary the subjects and methods of training. There are excellent manuals, films, and aids in many agencies which can be adapted for yours.

Another perspective

Perhaps the greatest asset in having volunteers is their perspective on services. As neither paid staff nor consumers, they can see things others don't notice; needs that aren't being met, duplications, and—most of all—new ideas, new ways to do things. With a share in partnership with both providers and consumers in planning, they may come up with ideas everyone can use. Nothing is quite so satisfying as seeing one's spontaneous ideas spark action and work out!

We are missing the boat if we don't involve volunteers in solving our problems. They develop commitment to the goals of the agency services and may have access to resources neither staff nor consumers can muster. Volunteers see it from a personal standpoint and can do a great deal to facilitate the use of service.

Most of all, what the volunteer offers is *time*—a commodity of which no staff member ever has enough. But if we are luring people into service from other pleasures, we have to make sure the service gives pleasures, too. Volunteer time is just as valuable as paid time—and should be taken just as seriously. Soon the volunteer is giving not only his time but his skills and his wisdom and a good part of himself. And that's a gift beyond measure.

18

Volunteer Careers

Volunteer careers count as qualifying experience toward paid work with the United States Civil Service and academically for the Educational Testing Service. The beauty of volunteer careers, unlike paid work, is the freedom the volunteer enjoys about what to do, with whom to do it, for how long and how deep will be the commitment. In paid careers these decisions are often taken out of our hands and necessity takes the reins. Another important contrast is in the primary obligations felt by each. The paid worker conscientiously contracts to give full time and top effort to the paid position, but the volunteer always has *other* primary obligations, such as family roles, or the source of support.

An important contrast is the volunteer's gift of discretionary time with the paid worker's sale of committed time. All humans receive time in equal quantities, but some have more discretionary time than others. The volunteer careerist is truly admirable for serving instead of choosing pleasure or unproductive activity. As a paid person I must admit to moments of stress when my work day is scheduled for several more hours, and I see a volunteer leave for a round of golf on a beautiful day or a flight to Florida on a nasty one. Then I remember how I use my free time, often humbled at the thought!

The choices involved are not always evident when the original decision is made. That's why recruitment lures, job descriptions, contracts and work habits need to be examined periodically to accommodate growth, and changes in the situation.

A volunteer career should be planned, just as a paid career is. There is a real continuous self-analysis process needed, before the

Presented for the Junior League Magazine Bicentennial Edition July 1976 decision is made and during systematic exploration through a progression of learning experiences on the job, and in retreat settings. As volunteer parochialism and turfdom barriers go down, there is now much more opportunity for learning through horizontal as well as vertical mobility for volunteers. Turnover is not bad, when one leaves a responsibility in good hands and strives to fulfill a higher one. Optimally, there's another someone with experience and wisdom to turn to for advice, someone who responds appreciatively, appreciation based on awareness of their growth, impact and accomplishments.

For years, the advocates for volunteer careers have claimed being a volunteer could yield just as much prestige and satisfaction as a professional career does. This is not to say "volunteer" and "professional" are opposites, for they definitely are not: many paid staff are not professional persons, and many professional persons apply all their skill, knowledge and art on an unpaid basis. Fortunately we count professionals of all conceivable disciplines among the volunteer ranks, because in this country we tend to define volunteer as a person who freely chooses to give service without compensation *quid pro quo*. We acknowledge all sorts of other rewards, but give payment for service rendered only to employees. Women no longer make a dichotomous choice of either marriage and children *or* a career. They move in and out of the labor market, often keeping up with their professions through volunteering in off periods.

The Classification Division of the Department of Labor clarified some important distinctions: a *profession* is an occupation unique in its societal function, usually organized into a body, self-disciplined by its value system and ethics, recognized for its members' special knowledge and competencies which can be transmitted by teaching to succeeding generations. Max Lerner in the Saturday Review last November had some scathing things to say about the disgrace of the professions in our changing world.[1]

He feels we are betrayed by some mal-practicing doctors, lawyers, and other disciplines more concerned with profit than with service. Such disenchantment is coloring everyone's feelings about professional associations, particularly the ardent idealistic young, who do

[1] "Watergating on Main Street" by Max Lerner, *Saturday Review* November 1, 1975 P. 10

not want to be perceived as profiteering at the expense of other persons, and don't join.

But we still mean as a tribute to character and to competence the compliment "a real professional" when we speak of an individual. It is in this spirit that Ellen Straus has written so eloquently about *The Professional Volunteer*. She means reliable, capable and quite as accountable for stewardship of resources, time and effort, as any salaried person. She emphasizes that the volunteer who can run a Call for Action Program is willing to have performance evaluated, impact measured, and a qualified analysis of cost/benefit ratios applied to the work accomplished because there is nothing to fear from a close look at what has been going on. And such a volunteer has no employment aspirations. The ACTION/Census Bureau study says only 2% of Americans who volunteered in 1974 were seeking employment.

Whether paid or not, the professional person to me is the one who places service above self-interest, who values people more than things, who cares about the reasons *why* more than *how-to's*. These values are not connected to the paycheck, but to the person and his attitudes about other people. One does not have to hang out a shingle and charge fees for service to be a professional, or to realize one's own fullest potential. Self-transcendence is the essence of maturity, and an ideal we can all strive for. When one's goals and objectives are for others, happiness is seeing those others enjoy them. An ego-centric search for personal happiness is hollow. Wise founding fathers guaranteed us the right to pursue it, not to have it! An altruistic pursuit is a higher human endeavor, and more rewarding.

Work classification experts have another concept which is important here: *professional work*.[2] This means work which can be done either for pay or for whatever intangible reward has meaning for the worker, who can be a volunteer or a paid person. Here the focus is on the advanced level of knowledge and skills required. Often academic credentials are to prove preparedness for intellectual and varied areas of skilled activity. The most interesting aspect of professional work is that it cannot be standardized into a con-

---

[2] US Dept. of Labor, Labor-Management Relations Division A/SMLR No. 170 pursuant to Sec. 6 of Executive Order # 11491.

sistent period of time, and must have individualized exercise of discretion and judgment in its performance. In my words, one is doing professional work when dealing with complex, dynamic situations in which there are so many variables to be considered that no one could give one right answer, a recipe or a road map to follow: the individual must decide, and live with the decision.

People are not born full blown professionals. It takes life-long learning, self-understanding and skill perfection, always alert to new developments which challenge previous knowledge and assumptions. One can spend a life time at a career for which there is payment in cash, or in which great achievement, fulfilling relationships and the power of expertise and skill are the only real rewards.

Dilettantes don't have a career, whether paid or not. It takes patience, grit, perseverance and a constant open-to-learning attitude, in any career, paid or not, to succeed. Without the simple reward system of pay, the motivation and retention of volunteers is much more complicated. We know that 62% of American workers are dissatisfied with their jobs, but no one has studied how many volunteers are.[1] We do know the dropout rates are not far apart during the first year. A paid worker may become a volunteer or vice versa, and many of us are both in different settings.

Many volunteers have said that full partnership with a paid staff counterpart is the greatest reward they receive, because it carries with it the gratifying knowledge that their work is essential to the team accomplishments. For others, they enjoy relationships with the people being served, and progress to overcome handicapping conditions. Finding like-minded people, working together on common problems toward shared goals, are most important to activists, rather than to the service oriented. A healthy democracy needs all three kinds of persons in the paid work force, and even more as volunteers.

As the concept of New Federalism is applied by many new laws, revenue sharing and decentralization of decision-making is devolving to local communities. Even the federal budget is now subject to citizen comments before adoption. Many local services are accountable to local people, not to "the Feds." Citizens are needed on advisory committees and boards in every human service field.

[1] *Work in America* HEW study of employment attitudes, 1972.

Legislation requires non-provider participation in health, welfare, mental health and educational planning in groups. Informed citizens who learn from service volunteering are those best prepared to advocate better service receiving systems[3] to dovetail with the delivery systems designed by the experts. Local citizens best understand their community and its needs.

The volunteer as change agent and "righter of wrongs" has less risk than victims of problems, or those who must keep their jobs in order to eat! This freedom of choice and freedom to take risks is very important, because the volunteer is known not to be paid to take a stand. Authentic because he seems to speak not in self-interest, but presumably out of altruism, he has credibility which both consumers and paid providers lack. We need all three perspectives in service planning and the advocate process. It will ultimately be the informed citizen volunteer who holds the balance of power when consumers and providers clash.

What greater aspirations could cap a volunteer career than making certain that human services are effective, targeted on priority needs and efficient? A career in that kind of work is the highest form of service—and the most needed perspective in our society today!

Career Lattice Enhances Volunteer Job Mobility

The U.S. Dept. of Labor's Division of Classification has accepted for entry in the new *Dictionary of Occupational Titles* a six-level career lattice for volunteer administrators proposed by the National center for Voluntary Action (NCVA).

The *Dictionary*, often used as the standard for government staff structure, qualifications, job ratings and pay, will list volunteer administrators as professional managers and technicians in the 1976 Bicentennial edition (see VAN, 4/74).

The career lattice was devised by Mrs. Harriet Naylor, former NCVA Director of Education and Training, during a series of meetings with Dept. of Labor representatives.

Duties: Mrs. Naylor pointed out that volunteer leadership involves all the duties of personnel administration—recruitment, work

[3]"Volunteer as Advocate" by Dr. Ivan Scheier at Association of Volunteer Bureaus Jubilee, Kansas City, May 3, 1976.

analysis, training and counseling, rewards, and record keeping/reporting—as well as tasks in public relations and program development.

The major payoff of the change in classification may be an increase in volunteer professionalism which would enable administrators to transfer laterally as well as vertically within the human services field.

Horizontal options: That is, administrators at each of the six levels may be able to assume jobs of roughly comparable responsibility at a number of human service agencies—government, schools, hospitals, public welfare, probation, museums, theatre organizations—and hold marketable, well-defined skills common to them all. The career lattice can reach from small local programs to national ones, with horizontal options all along the way.

The Career Lattice

The "steps" in the career lattice are as follows:

Director of Volunteer Services—The chief paid administrator of a volunteer services department, the Director is part of top administration, and usually reports directly to the executive of the organization.

The Director plans, develops and implements policies, standards and procedures of volunteer participation; plans and organizes volunteer orientation and training; manages the central office, including staffing and record-keeping; develops and directs the budget; promotes public relations and education; participates in professional meetings.

The Director must have experience and education equivalent to a master's degree, plus three years' administration or supervisory experience.

Asst. Director of Volunteer Services—Under direction of the Director, the Asst. Director carries particular delegated responsibilities. The position requires the equivalent of a master's degree, plus one year administrative or supervisory experience.

Program Director—Under direction of the Director, the Program Director carries delegated responsibilities with special service emphasis (e.g., RSVP, Student Volunteers, etc.).

Presented in the Voluntary Action News published by the National Center for Voluntary Action Washington D.C. June 1974

Coordinator of Volunteer Services—Under direction of the Director, the Coordinator administers a division within a complex organization. The Coordinator plans, develops and implements policies and standards within the division, and manages recruitment, orientation, evaluation and recognition of volunteers in that unit.

Asst. Coordinator of Volunteer Services—Under direction of the Coordinator, the Asst. Coordinator carries particular delegated responsibilities.

Supervisor of Volunteers—The Supervisor directly supervises volunteers in a particular project or work area and makes evaluative input to the program development and planning process. Working with staff and community groups as assigned, the Supervisor plans and carries out operational responsibilities as assigned, develops specific volunteer assignments, recruits volunteers for those tasks, trains staff and keeps records of donations and services.

19

Volunteers in Welfare

It is rare, even on a day in June, to find a state Welfare Department staff meeting with the theme "Bloom and Grow", I suppose because your Commissioner is named Flowers. But the recognition that we all work at quite lonely roles surrounded by other kinds of people means that when we get a rare chance to get together, we have much to teach and to learn from one another. In these spectacular natural surroundings—as my husband used to say when we lived and worked here, "Let the Swiss have their Alps, I'll take West Virginia"—the natural ingenuity and mutual supportiveness of the mountaineers needs just a little help to be channeled where it is most needed, and that's what our work is all about. Sue Beard and I were talking about this on the way over, and I learned a name for this unique capacity to accomplish a great deal with little expenditure of money. She said you all are expert at "cobbling", and I think your cobbling can be an inspiring model for our new profession of volunteer administration. I intend to "brag on you" as I travel over the rest of the country.

You have come with some very good examples of how you have coped with increasing demands for volunteer services, and I'm sure with some very specific questions about how to do your job better. We will spend most of our time in small groups where you can share experiences and ways to "cobble". I sure hope to start you off by bringing up some of the questions which we are facing in other fields where volunteers are active, and asking you to help us raise competency among coordinators and the volunteers with whom they work. Volunteering is no casual, sometime thing, but a very important supplement to what the paid staff can do, and leader-

Presented to the Area Coordinators of Volunteer Services of West Virginia on June 7, 1974

ship of volunteers is no simple task. Newcomers to the field always assume that getting volunteers is the big problem, but you and I know, its *keeping* them that's hard, building their ability to do important things, and their desire to stick with hard jobs until they accomplish something they can be proud of!

Dr. David Horton Smith, a sociologist, has spent a lot of time observing volunteering and volunteer administration, analyzing what is happening and thinking about the great potential resource volunteers represent. He agrees with me that we are only scratching the surface of that potential now, while our problems multiply faster than we can solve them. Indeed, sometimes solving one problem just creates a whole set of new ones. Automobiles get people around faster and more efficiently than horses or oxen, but look what they do to the atmosphere, the beauty and even the safety of the countryside. Dr. Smith is interested in us, the practitioners of volunteer administration. He has watched us struggle to learn the how to's of recruitment, training, record keeping, etc., which he calls techniques. At meetings like this one, this is often the kind of information we share, and that learning is very valuable. Over the past twenty-odd years I have been one of the experimenters in developing techniques. I think we have worked out ways—technology, which David Horton Smith calls the second stage of becoming a professional. And our technology is tried and true—it works. But before we go much further, we have to stop and ask ourselves some "whys". We are in danger of getting pretty good at doing something which could be used for good or for bad ends. We can be used by other people for their goals, if we don't watch out, if we don't have some good and valid reasons for goals of our own. Only when we have given careful thought to our reasons why, should we set our goals.

One reason we need to express our goals clearly is that the people who pay the bills need to understand what it is we are trying to do. I was delighted to learn that your Commissioner has talked about the meaning of the word "welfare," and that he sees it as the writers of the Constitution of the United States saw it: with a small w, well-being of all the people, not what it has come to mean with a capital W, a dole of goods and money to the poor, which bears such a stigma we have to be very careful to keep secret the names of those who need it. So one of the most important reasons for what we do as volunteer administrations is the *need*, and sometimes we have some very tough decisions about which need is more important than which other one. That's why we ourselves need to involve other people in some of our decision-making, to get other perspectives and understand what is important to other people, not just staff convenience, or expediency. The law, and then the regulations and the budget set very important limits on what we can do. That's why we want our bosses with us in our decisions. We are subject to pressures from other staff, and we want to get along with them as well as we can, but their needs are not the primary concern for us, either. Our skills must be applied to matching client or program needs to the needs of volunteers. Much as the transactional analysts have discovered, we have found that it works out quite well when we can find complementary needs and match them. Some of the most striking examples of this come in Foster Grandparent or Foster Grand Child Programs. In our society, not many families live with three generations together. But older persons need a meaningful role in life and relationship to young people. Students who have "adopted" older neighbors for whom they can do small chores and errands find a great deal of wisdom, patience and time to take an interest from the older persons they help. A good volunteer placement has resources for mutual satisfaction.

The matching process in volunteer placement has been too lightly glossed over: often the first volunteer to walk into our office after a request is received is the person sent to fill it, with too little attention paid to how it will fit. A principle has evolved to guide us, and that is that the wider the range of choice offered the volunteer, the more likely he is to feel well placed when he decides which assignment to accept. But there is a more universal principle involved in the very meaning of volunteering: freedom of choice, not only for the volunteer, but for all the other people involved in the new relationship: the worker who happens to be paid should make the decision and not feel obligated to accept or keep every volunteer who offers to help him. Most important is giving the client some choice, as well. No one should be left with the awful feeling of having been coerced into a voluntary relationship. Yet sometimes under time or urgency pressures this happens, and volunteering gets the bad name the word has in the military. This is precisely what Webster says volunteerism is *not* supposed to mean.

The volunteer director is accountable for the quality of the relationships and placements which are worked out, for the best possible use of the time and talents which are offered by citizens, just as much as for the tangible contributions which may be involved. The volunteers have a right to optimum placements, and then an obligation to carry out the appropriate responsibilities involved. No matter how highly qualified they are when they come to us, volunteers need orientation to the situation in which they will find themselves, information about the ground rules under which they will serve, the people with whom they will work, and the resources they can turn to, for help or advice. Like paid staff, they are equally deserving of an honest appraisal of their work and its impact. In fact, certainty that their work is important to other people is very important in retaining volunteers. I have often heard administrators say that a certain program could not operate without volunteers—the Superintendent of Schools in Louisville, Kentucky said this about his whole school system. My hope is that this be more often said earnestly *to the volunteers* themselves, for I consider that the highest form of "pay" we can give volunteers. Other forms of recognition are fine. After all, like everything else we do for volunteers, recognition must be tailored to them as unique individuals, different from everyone else in the world. But to know "I am absolutely essential," not just tolerated, means a lot to most of us. Having seen the pictures of your volunteer of the year this year, I can imagine what fun it was to communicate such appreciation to that dear little girl. (Ed. note: An eighteen-months-old AFDC child visits the elderly regularly with her mother, and received the West Virginia Volunteer of the Year Award!)

So, freedom of choice for all the people involved is one obligation for us to guarantee, and recognition of the absolute uniqueness of people is another. These lead to a very demanding third obligation, that of making recommendations, counselling staff and volunteers and making decisions *with* them, not *for* them. Ability to do that is of the highest order, which is why many of us were so concerned when we found out that our new profession was being classified as "miscellaneous clerical" by the Census Bureau in 1970. Last Fall, we were given assurances by the Chief Classification Officer of the US Dept. of Labor that we will be classified in the highest work orders "professional, technical and managerial" when the new Dictionary of Occupational Titles, the definition authority, comes out as part of the Bicentennial. I think the fact that we deal with the good side of the nature of man, that we see people at their best, altruistic, self-trancendent, feeling good about themselves, has been what has kept us going when only *we* knew how important our work is. There's a lesson in that experience which we should use in working with volunteers and other staff—let them know how important they are, and how much appreciated!

What I've been talking about are *values*, the things we come to realize are terribly important, are good, and which we use as guidelines in our decision-making. I recently found out that work is considered professional when it requires very special decision-making, decisions which cannot be standardized but must be derived from consideration of the many factors involved which are variables: goals, resources, readiness and timing. Our professional judgments about these factors determine the validity of our decisions. The invariables involved are the values contained in our beliefs and code of ethics: what we uphold with integrity under all sorts of pressures. I hope in our learning we will deal not only with techniques, with analyzing how to's into a technology of management, but also with a personal philosophy which will help us make sound and ethical decisions, because our effectiveness depends much more on what kind of persons we are than on what we know how to do!

We need to ask ourselves honestly whether we really believe in people, trust volunteers, think they are needed. What can we do to preserve the dignity and integrity of our clients, our volunteers and the rest of the staff? Charles Truax, well known in the rehabilitation field has defined three essentials for the helping person: genuineness, non-possessive warmth (not to encourage dependence on us, but maturity enough to release people to greater independence, and enjoyment of mutual inter-dependence) and accurate empathy, really seeing the person's problem as he sees it. It has been said that a problem is not a problem unit it involves us personally—and we ourselves have to accept the reality of our clients' problems, and help our volunteers to see them this way, too. Years ago, we worried about our volunteers becoming "too involved" but we are beginning to see that it is that very involvement which actually makes them effective helpers—they really *care*, and that is a motivating force for our clients to make better use of the services which can be provided.

The caseworkers and line staff are responsible for planning the services delivery system. Our responsibility as volunteer administrators is to involve our volunteers and give leadership to the way volunteers can facilitate *receiving systems* to maximize the effectiveness of the services delivered. We are being pressed to set up realistic and measurable goals, which is a very difficult thing to do when we deal with so many intangibles. But we are going to have to communicate with an economist dominated society to get support for volunteer activities, and that means we shall have to be able to prove that we and our volunteers are worth the administrative investment it takes to have them. Just counting heads, or even just counting hours served tells us very little about the worth of the time spent volunteering. We have very little research to back up our observations over the years, but I have faith that we are going to be able to prove that worth when we realize how important it is. Remember, it has been aptly said that an economist is a fellow who knows the price of everything but the value of nothing. We are the people responsible now for proving the value of volunteering now if our society is to benefit from volunteers in the future.

20

On Becoming a Profession

In the almost ten years of membership I have enjoyed in this organization, I have come almost full circle in my thinking about forming a new profession. When I first joined, I found people expressing great frustration that their profession was not recognized, and using the name as though wishing would make it so. I have always coveted for the Volunteer Administrator recognition for the high degree of competency the work demands, access to high level policy staff decision making, and commensurate compensation for the work performed, so often far beyond the hours, effort and personal commitment of any of the other so called helping professions which surround us.

In fact, I am reminded of the non-verbal short film called "Joshua in the Box". We are boxed in on four sides: by the designated authority for whom we work at the top, volunteers and the whole community on one side, and the paid line and supervisory staff on the other side, with all of us depending on and trying to meet the needs of some client group as our reason for existence and source of pressure from the fourth side of the box. Needs have some identified characteristics which give people a label like patient, inmate, resident—whatever the euphemism, there is usually in our heartless society some stigma implied. And here we are in the box, pressed in by one side after another, or all at once, trying to keep our heads when all about us are losing theirs. Joshua ends the film with a great wide-mouthed shriek, the lips finally becoming the edges of the box. There he is sitting in a corner, thinking things over. And that is where I think AAVSC is today: thinking things over.

I see us having developed a body of readily transmissible tech-

Presented to the American Association of Volunteer Services Coordinators Annual Meeting Denver, Colorado September 1974 niques, which can be taught in a number of ways so that newcomers can learn quite quickly how to do our work of recruiting, training, referring, and record keeping—all the technical stuff we do. These are the things that our new members come to meetings and training workshops to get. We have sat down in a corner to think at these meetings before. I remember as one of our best speakers Dr. Bob Lee of Southern Illinois, begged us to recognize a personal responsibility to take time for "putsying", I think he called it—sorting out ideas, facing new issues, getting things into perspective so that we can react rationally, not just hysterically from one crisis to another. To me, he was saying that being professional is being disciplined, self-disciplined, so that one gives his best thinking to his work. In that sense we are not yet a profession, but we have made a start at becoming one.

In my work with Personnel Administrators, particularly the job classification people, in trying to get the work upgraded from the miscellaneous clerical category into which the Census Bureau relegated us in 1970, I have learned the importance of understanding professional work, a professional person, a profession and a professional association. I have learned what we are expected to do, our role is professional work. Not all incumbents, however, are professional persons. We are working hard through our association to develop status for the profession in the eyes of the rest of the world: to deserve the trust of the public to be competent for a unique service.

The Department of Labor which is by law the source of definitions about work which are then applied by other people, has a definition of professional work which is a real challenge: work is considered professional when the decisions it requires cannot be standardized like the relationships and laws of physical science, or even a recipe in a cookbook or a road map—there are too many variables, all reacting in dynamic relation to the others, which must be analysed and kept in balance in the decisions. Our judgments are made in a world of confusion and ambiguity, and constant change. Such work is not clerical, for sure, though we have to admit it certainly is miscellaneous: Volunteers are unique individuals, each with a different self-concept and his own experiences, feelings, home situation, work obligations, ideals, objectives and degree of interest and commitment. There are the same kinds of differences among the paid staff and the clients with whom we all work. Then how in the world do we make rational, disciplined decisions which will match people to the assignment best for all concerned?

The answer lies, I believe, in our own value system: what we think is good, important, worthwhile, likely to advance us toward good goals and objectives. Gone are the days when we simply tried to please everyone, because we found that is simply impossible. So we have to think through very seriously what yardsticks we will use in our own individual decision-making, what values will be our guidelines as professional persons, what criteria will determine our professional behavior. Some of these values have their roots in our religious and cultural heritage. With growing pride in ethnicity, we can no longer count on the melting pot to abolish differences. We hardly realize how much the kind of person we are determines the kind of professional person we can be, and the way we perceive other people. MacGregor in his X and Y theory of managers touched on this very sensitive area, and like the arguments about heredity and environment, there are theorists who believe that people cannot change from being untrusting, controlling, authoritarian leaders into democratic, optimistic leaders with faith in the possibility of learning to change. As a trainer, I must admit that the job is much easier with the positivist than the X type person, but it is greater satisfaction to see him begin to develop trust, test some positive approaches, and become more democratic in his behavior.

Every group needs some skeptics and devil's advocates who think deeper than a pietistic acceptance. A danger with the Y type person is that he may not test his assumptions to make sure they are true in a given instance, and then he feels really betrayed, and loses some faith in his fellowman when he is disappointed.

Professional discipline demands that we test our assumptions, validate our information, and make decisions based on facts, as much as possible, not hunches or prejudices! The real pro recognized how many differences there can be in the way people see the same thing, and takes responsibility to clarify these differences, instead of glossing them over. Who knows? What we believed to be true yesterday may be proved untrue tomorrow—we must be open to new ideas and information, and not guided by obsolete assumptions.

Part of our flexibility depends on how much opportunity we have had for formal learning, because adult educators have proved that the more education a person has had, the more likely he is to seek more. I believe, and would like to see research prove, that we can say the same thing about training. In the meantime, we who seek to be known as professional persons will be perceived that way by other persons if we seize every learning opportunity we can, and work to create more, in the belief that learning is a life-long process.

Having gone through two earlier identity crises, one in becoming a social worker, and the second in becoming also an adult educator, I have watched the struggles of both those disciplines to gain recognition as meeting the criteria for being a profession. At the recent AVAS meeting, where discussion centered around bringing all the professional volunteer administrators together in some sort of umbrella organization, strong feelings emerged about loyalty to special fields of practice, such as schools, corrections, hospitals. In response to some of the scathing things being said about competition and turfdom, one thoughtful older social worker who had lived through the merger of all social workers into one organization brought the discussion up to a new level by pointing out that that merger had not achieved the millenium. Much of the enthusiasm and spontaneity in program and services development had been lost, since no one could become quite so devoted to the "generic" social worker concept as people had been to child welfare, or psychiatric case work, etc. She urged us not to lose such enthusiasm in AAVSC, and I concur in that warning. Enthusiasm and spontaneity are important in all human services, but especially so in the volunteer world, where we have fewer ways to reward people. If the professional people stop enjoying their work, and being inspired by their professional organization, this will affect their volunteers very quickly. Let's be sure that we let prospective members know that we anticipated the need for special interest groups by providing for them when 100 members want their own section.

As a profession we could go the scientific route, as librarians did. But I know some librarians who like their books on the shelves better than borrowed. Let's not become a union, interested most in our pay or prestige, either. Let's just improve our services.

Somehow, we have to enjoy the richness of our diversity while uniting around common goals and objectives. We must remember what Marlene Wilson has taught us about the relationship between energy release and appropriateness of goals. What are the common goals of volunteer administration? I believe they must be important to our country and to all people, not just ourselves, or just volunteers. If doctors are concerned with health, and lawyers with justice as their ideal, then I believe our potential profession is concerned with freedom of choice, by definition of voluntarism. We have not always behaved this way—we have knuckled under to our bosses, to staff pressures, to powerful volunteers. If you doubt what this means, how many recipients of volunteer services have been given a choice? How many of our manuals or by-laws for auxiliaries have mentioned freedom? Yet, I believe *freedom* is our responsibility, else we are vulnerable to charges of "using" volunteers, of band-aiding serious community needs.

If we are to deserve the privileges of being entrusted as professional persons, we shall have to take a deeper and broader vision of the significance of volunteer work to the volunteer, to the recipient, to the agency and to the whole community. We ought to be leaders in the community, not simply suppliers of free labor. We could be developing volunteering as a route out of powerlessness for our recipients. We should defend the right to volunteer, and work with our fellow coordinators to find the broadest possible range of choice for volunteers, in the kinds of work they could do and the influence they could have on new programming and policy development. As Revenue Sharing and Advisory Committees are being formed, we should have competent volunteers with first-hand experience in our programs, ready to serve. Otherwise, the people needing services and the consumers will stand as adversaries and progress will be blocked. Just as volunteers enrich and extend services, they can broaden the perspectives and mediate in community decision-making groups. They are sorely needed, and we are the people who know who they are and what they could do. If we free them to take on such broad responsibilities, we will have ambassadors from our services all over town. Volunteering is just about the best learning method I know—and we in this new profession set the ceiling on what is being learned. We must encourage and cooperate with research, and apply the findings. We have a tremendous stake in the encouragement of educational curriculum and cooperation with educators in our communities. A profession must have a body of sound knowledge which can be taught. We are having the experiences which demonstrate the areas that knowledge should embrace, and we have the resources to help test theories and prove hypotheses.

Most important of all, probably, is that we have contact with all kinds of people in a community, and can bring them together over common concerns as few other professions can. It is only through wide voluntary involvement that our community problems can be attacked. Sometimes solving one creates others, and some problems can only be made more bearable, defying solution. But the quality of life in a problem-solving community is far preferable to that in one where problems are hidden, denied, or avoided. Our ethics are based on our individual value systems, but they must be explicit as well as demonstrated in our professional behavior. I should like to suggest we devote meeting times in the future to some of the democratic values which freedom implies, which volunteering can strengthen:

1. Broader participation in program development and policy making by volunteers
2. Developing better evaluation of the effect of volunteering on volunteers as citizens, on "clients", on community life
3. Respecting the dignity and integrity of each person involved
4. Influencing public policy about human needs priorities: people are more important than things
5. Current issues without easy answers: voluntary organization support under current tax limits, for example
6. How to express our accountability to various audiences for the gifts of time, effort and resources which are entrusted to us, in terms they understand according to *their* value systems.

Human beings have a way of escaping into technical discussions when the subjects at hand become too uncomfortable. Surely we can meet some learning needs of new practitioners at our meetings through seminars and workshops. But if we are to become a respected professional association, we shall have to face squarely some of the criticism being leveled at volunteering, instead of just hoping it will go away. In times of rising prices, the time and efforts which we direct where they are most needed become more valuable than ever, and waste more serious. To me, our responsibility is very, very serious. We are the gatekeepers for one of the last places in our society in which it is ok to be compassionate, to express sympathy and concern—and we control to whom these expressions shall be directed. We used to worry about "letting volunteers get too involved". Now we know that it is their very involvement which makes the difference, their compassion (their feeling *with* the other fellow) which restores his self respect and motivation to try to overcome his problem. This is an awesome responsibility, but one which makes life worth living. As duChardin put it so beautifully,

"When man has conquered the wind and the wave, the stars and the forces of gravity, and turns to release the power of love, for God, mankind for the second time will have discovered fire"

21

Creative Use of Volunteers

I've been asked to talk to you about the creative use of volunteers and those of you who worked with me remember that I don't agree that we use volunteers. I think we're being attacked from many quarters for that word "use". So I hope as we think together how to keep volunteers, we can consider that they are free, autonomous individuals who have a right not to be used, but to be given an opportunity to do something important and to put in their own point of view about what we're doing in such a way that we enrich and extend the programs that we believe in.

It seems to me that in the old days we used to be able to turn a volunteer loose and there were so few of them that we could monitor each one without worrying about how that volunteer's behavior might affect our system. Those chaotic days are over and I think now we are recognizing that unless we bring some order out of chaos and channel the energies of volunteers effectively, they are not happy in their work and they don't stay with us very long. We need to work out a system within our program which takes care of the needs of volunteers from the beginning of their experience with us as long as they want to serve.

I think it's terribly important we recognize the definition of the volunteer, which has such words in the dictionary as spontaneity, freedom from coersion, free will and most of all, free choice. Therefore, in using volunteers we must give volunteers this freedom and like any other freedom it has with it responsibility and self-discipline for the individual in order that

Presented at the Telephone Lecture Network Volunteer Services Lecture Series January 16, 1975 he not encroach on the rights of other people. Our job then is to figure out our program goals and then the goals for each of the people within it, combing out those things that are appropriate for volunteers to do which staff perhaps used to do or which may have been spontaneously thought up by the volunteers themselves, as long as they're consistent with what everybody else is trying to do and working to improve and reinforce the program.

The first point, I think, is for volunteers to think through the objectives for the work that we assign them. This means that we have to have given them manageable units of work which are going to be an attractive and meaningful opportunity to do something worthwhile. Gone are the days when volunteers were satisfied to do the "mickey-mouse" kinds of things that staff didn't want to be bothered with. Now we have to recognize because of their freedom volunteers are able to do things that nobody on the staff can do, partly because they come to us from a network of connections in the community and they have access to resources that we can never tap from a staff position.

Most of the helping professions need advocates. In our culture today which is dominated by economists and people who think in terms of cost benefit, all of the intangible values that volunteers bring need to be described and interpreted to the general public, and that's what I mean when I talk about volunteer advocacy. We on the staff have to come to realize that probably no staff person should do anything a volunteer could do. Because with the tight budgets today, it's impossible ever to create paid jobs for everything that would be beneficial to the patients. Our analysis of the program that we have, its objectives, must include those things which cannot be budgeted but which are terribly important to the people we serve.

Another point that we must consider is the accurate placement of volunteers that will tap the interests and the motivation of that volunteer. We will talk about motivation, not in the sense that we can motivate anybody else, but that we can create the conditions which will motivate people under their own steam. When I talk about freedom with responsibility and discipline,

I'm not talking only about professional persons, I'm talking about every volunteer who has a clear sense of purpose in the job we give him and recognizes the limitations on that work which are necessary because of the setting in which he is working or the laws which pertain to what he does. Therefore, he has some understanding that he has to get from the program which no amount of formal education will have given him. In churches they talk about our "givens", the conditions that we find ourselves in over which we have no control. I think as staff members we have strong feelings about not being able to control more of what happens to us on our jobs. Volunteers have the same feeling and in the competition today for volunteers, they're going to go where they feel they can do something important and that they are free to carry the message of the needs of our patients out from us and the program itself into all of the groups that they associate with and the rest of their lives. We're thinking now of volunteer advocacy as terribly important in order to create better community conditions for our patients. The more ambassadors about mental health we can create in the community, the more support there will be for the programs we believe in. By keeping volunteers out, staff lose the possibility of having ambassadors about the value of the staff work and the value of the program.

When we're recruiting volunteers, it's a very different ball game from years ago when it was considered the virtuous thing to do for certain people already quite privileged. Now we're thinking that volunteering is so good for people that we've got to provide opportunities for all kinds of people to be volunteers. And this means that our old patterns of screening, of training, and of recognition are not appropriate for all the different kinds of people who are willing to help if they understand why we need them.

There are some people in our society who are organizing against volunteering, particularly service volunteering. The National Organization of Women is saying that volunteering has been one of the ways women have been held down and to some extent, they're right. As long as we *use* volunteers, and do not give them an opportunity to get into the program planning process, setting goals, helping us design delivery systems for services, and most of all, interpreting to us the service receiving system from the point of view of the community, we're vulnerable to that charge from the N.O.W. organization. Fortunately we don't have the staff in the mental health field organizing to keep volunteers out, but we do have some units of organized labor who are developing labor contracts to keep volunteering out. I believe this is because the budget pressures are so great; jobs are being eliminated. This is for real. And we have to be awfully sure that we are not using volunteers to prevent people from getting jobs. Even economists are telling us that what we do in providing jobs for volunteers may eliminate entry-level jobs for people who are marginally employable. Therefore, we have to be awfully certain that we're not bandaiding old systems, but involving volunteers as individuals in developing new systems which are going to meet better the needs of patients. This means a whole new understanding about scheduling in order to be able to use people who work, after 5:00 p.m. and weekends. There are a great many opportunities for people to help patients, to develop public understanding in support of our programs on their own time which do not happen between 9:00 and 5:00. We need to have staff available for these people to get back to if they need help at all hours and not necessarily limit volunteering to staff convenience but to focus on the needs of patients and the availability of volunteers.

We haven't tapped people in families as volunteers. More and more we are finding that a family can perform services on behalf of people within the home by taking children on a respite visit or by taking an older person so that other people can regroup their forces and be ready to take better care of that person after a visit in a private home. We are not using businesses and industries as corporate citizens nearly as much as we could. Many businesses are willing to loan their art departments or their public relations people to help us to develop brochures, posters, and art work for displays. We ought to be sending letters to the personnel departments of corporations when we have a special need. Many of us have people and industry are accustomed to phasing, in system terms.

Many corporations will help us work out a schedule for a new volunteer which will give that person the learning he needs in the beginning so that he can quickly be effective in our programs. Some have training facilities and are willing to help us in many ways that we have not tapped, in addition to supplying their employees on a release-time basis as individuals or in groups for projects that we might need.

How are we going to get the disadvantaged people in as volunteers? It's not part of their life-style but it's a terribly important human experience for these people. We cannot simply wait for them to come to us to offer to volunteer. We must develop a network of people in the community who believe in what we're doing and who will help private citizens see what they can do within our program. This means a real soul-searching by all the staff involved in a program before you get the first volunteer and periodically afterwards.

I think probably most of your programs have had an Advisory Committee of the staff and some community leaders for some time. My plea to you now is to involve experienced volunteers who are still in service roles in that group. Volunteers can look at all programs from a neutral point of view. The people who are providing the service are so busy they hardly ever have time to look at the whole picture. And the patients themselves who are now coming into our planning process have needs so important to them that sometimes they can't see the whole picture either. So it's important to get volunteers into this work analysis process in the very beginning and then define jobs in such a way that we have a certain kind of volunteer in mind and plan our recruiting to get that kind of person. This means that we can use the mass media. Actually that reaches more people than any other way of recruiting. But it doesn't say to a potential volunteer "I am the one who is needed because I am a special person." So I think we have to figure out where the kinds of people we need are in communities with the help of the volunteers we have planning with us and then how we're going to find those persons they know to link them into our programs.

How do we teach the volunteer what he needs to know in order to be effective? As part of the materials you were given in preparation for this lecture, you have a paper that says at the top "Planning for Training" and it shows a kind of "bullseye." (see illustration on page 89) My plea to you in looking at this is to see that the person is at the center of that. Some people have said have said arbitrarily that in education, formal education in primary and secondary schools and colleges, all learning is centered on what the people need to know and not nearly enough on the people themselves. That's why you see the word "self" in the center. This is the person, who he thinks he is, and what he wants to do, how he sees his former experience as useful in a new job. That's the next area that he needs to examine. So we need to have a person look at himself and why he was chosen and then at the job and what it requires.

That job may seem pretty formidable at first, so we don't give him the whole dose before he ever starts it, but we center on him and what he already knows how to do with part of that job and let him have some success. I'm saying that this learning process for volunteers has to be a continuous process and that we fare much better if we build small pieces of learning on a continuing basis rather than a long, arduous course during which the volunteer doesn't know what he needs to know and he will not remember the things that are most important to him. We build around the person, what he needs to know, about his job, the place where he's going to work, the other people in it and what they do, the organization as a whole; if it's a community service, it's a different kind of organization from a hospital. If it's designed for all kinds of people then the needs of those people have to be described in ways that the volunteer can see what he has that he can give which will help to meet those needs.

Finally, whether your program is in a community or in an institution, you certainly have to know your community and you have to recognize how much your volunteer knows about the community. I'm saying that in the orientation process, we take the person out from himself into ever-widening circles of concern, in a progressive learning process, so he can ask questions along the way. We create a climate in which it's safe to ask questions. It's o.k. to ask. And then because there are constant changes in all of these levels of concern: in the community, in the needs of the people being served within the organization and the way the work is divided in the organization, we have to get that information back to the volunteer continuously, so that he can see what that means to him. Those of you who were in the mental health field years ago when tranquilizers first came in know how much that technological change finally meant to everybody in the whole mental health system. And the volunteers were the last to find out what it meant to volunteering. I'm pleading that whenever there are changes we bring people together whose jobs ought to be changed because of some change somewhere else in the system and we give them a chance to test the meaning of this to them in their work.

Another important factor that is becoming more essential all the time, because people move from volunteer roles into paid roles and back again, is our record-keeping system. It is terribly important for volunteers to be able to document their volunteer experience with us, the training that they have had. The Educational Testing Service at Princeton, New Jersey which does college board exams and things like that is now developing examinations which will help volunteers prove what they have learned as volunteers and get college credit for it. The Adult Education Association is working on giving academic credit for the training that people have taken which has been given by organizations—not colleges. This means that a volunteer's training record and work experience record is a terribly important document for that volunteer and the least that we owe him in exchange for the service he gives us. I think it also means that some of the things that we used to worry so much about, which are concerned with hours of service and categories of service, are no longer useful in the form we had. We've got to think through who needs to know—maybe five years from now—and then develop a record system which will provide that information for the organization, for its records, for the staff about how much supervisory experience they have had which may be very meaningful to them in promotion times, and for the volunteers themselves so that they can see what changes they have seen in themselves from their volunteer experience.

It's terribly important than volunteers feel free in their jobs and not trapped, that we don't leave people in the same job forever but we provide mobility so that they can try another thing to do once they have had success. They may want to move upward to administrative roles, training or recruiting or being speechmakers for us, but others may prefer to stay in direct patient contact service roles and that is their choice. The point is that we don't keep them forever in one spot because they are ambassadors in the community and they need to understand our total program and to have as wide an experience as possible. When we're talking about volunteers in groups like this, we lose some of the meaning of the fact that they are all unique individual persons, no one of them is like any other one.

As we talk about meeting the needs of our patients, I think we should look for the needs of the volunteers which match the needs of the patients in some way so that if we can create a job for a volunteer in which he has certain needs and the patient has certain needs which can be met by the volunteer, then we're going to have the kind of volunteer experience which is going to keep a volunteer in our system and have him going out of it to talk about his life experiences. In a positive way, he becomes the ambassador we're talking about.

Another piece of paper that you have among your materials for this day is a very rough diagram like a triangle which is Maslow's pyramid of human needs. I'm sure you've all heard a lot about physical, psychological, social, ego and actualization needs. Maslow's idea was that until you satisfy the lowest levels, you cannot even be concerned about the higher levels. Psychologists are now challenging this idea and feeling that these needs persist throughout life. It's terribly important for us to look at all of these needs which all human beings have. The self-actualization one is the one I'd like to talk about primarily because to me this means the fullest development of every person to his greatest potential. I'm talking about patients, I'm talking about staff, I'm talking about volunteers.

In his later writings before his death, Maslow spoke of self-actualization really becoming self-transcendence. All the religions in the world have seen this truth: he who would find himself must lose himself in something greater. I think this is possible for volunteers in volunteering. One of the reasons that volunteering is a good thing for patients is it helps them to be interested and concerned about others as much as they are about themselves. I hope that this is the kind of volunteering which is truly creative volunteering for *all* persons and that we can give them satisfaction for this very high level human need.

Among other psychologists, Ericson has talked about different needs that people have at different stages of life. And in the second diagram is a line which goes from birth to death, we see that childhood has a different set of needs. Ericson speaks of these as developmental needs and for childhood this is for learning: it is very important that children be given information and the experience they need in order to be able to cope.

As we move into youth, there are other needs which begin to be more important than learning. We've all seen good students in primary grades become slightly less good students in high school because of their need to understand members of the opposite sex and to get along with them; their social needs become more important than the early needs that they felt as children: to please their peers and adults, to be safe, and so on. If you could visualize that triangle on its side, one psychiatrist in the Illinois system says that children's needs are primarily physical and youth's psychological, young adults—social, and middle-age and later middle-age are primarily ego needs—who are they, what do they do, what is their importance as individual persons. And that only in later years do we really actualize all the potential we have, and fewer people get to the higher level.

Now this is just a way of looking at people which applies to all people. Older people have lost some of the meaningful roles that they had. They have tremendous ego needs which they cannot meet through their work because they are retired; they have to find other ways to meet those needs. That's why, to give an older person a job which is not clearly defined, if he doesn't see why it's important, is simply making him feel worse about himself. But if he is given a role like "foster grandparent" he understands it is terribly important to another person, we're really meeting some of his very basic needs. I'm suggesting that after this lecture you analyze yourself first. Where are you in this life span and how are your very basic needs being met? Because you see there is a theory that unless our own needs are met, we aren't very able to respond to the needs of other people. Certainly we don't understand the needs of other people well if we don't really know ourselves. Go through the steps in the exercise and try analyzing yourself about all of these common needs that all human beings have and where you are.

As a person in later middle age, in fact, eligible to be considered for the American Association of Retired Persons, I have to recognize that I have very different needs from what I had several years ago, and I am under pressure as a wage earner and taxpayer. This is the age group that is busiest in its vocation and carrying the greatest tax burden, is carrying the responsibility for young people and their education, is the parent to their own parents. So I think sometimes when we limit volunteering to the traditional volunteer, the later middle-age female, we don't realize how many other pressures that person is under and that may be why the "lady bountiful", middle-aged, middle-sized volunteer is disappearing from the volunteer scene; she has escaped into paid employment because of the pressures or she is simply not willing to volunteer because there is already too much pressure in life. Look at yourself and then try applying this understanding to people whom you're interviewing in order to understand their needs and find a likely place for them to serve. Practice on people who are your friends. Tell them what you are doing; they may be very much interested in this kind of self-analysis and it may help them as it has helped me not feel guilty about not doing some things when I realize that because of my personal needs and the priorities that I have to set in my life I'm no longer able to do some of the things I used to enjoy.

The next material that you have in your hands is called "Who Wants to Volunteer?" I think in analyzing people we can do it by groups and I've suggested about six on this list: youth, people who work from 9:00 to 5:00 (this is probably the older young adult and middle-age people), students, older persons, clients, patients, and so on, and I want to stress the professional person. There's a lot of talk today in the volunteer field about professional volunteers. As you know I've been trying to professionalize the job of the volunteer coordinator for years and I wish we would stop trying to professionalize volunteers until we get a profession of our own.

There are many professional persons who are willing to give their service and if we can quibble about definitions, I would like to say that we have not tapped the needs of professional persons to do something without getting paid for it, and use their highest level of skills. Social workers, doctors who are retired, dentists, any number of professions, engineers (I remember Linda Hawley's engineers from one of the large corporations in Syracuse who fixed the television sets at Syracuse Psychiatric Institute—she called them the 'brownies' because they worked at night). This was professional volunteering to me; using the best skills you have from your own discipline in a situation where you're more free to do what you want to do. I'm thinking of retired teachers who find it very satisfying to work with people with learning disabilities. It challenges the very best of their training and it is the kind of volunteering that gives services which we never could afford in our budgets.

Let's individualize ourselves as administrators, the staff members with whom we work and the volunteers as well as the patients or clients with whom they're working. This means having tremendous respect for the life style and situation of each individual. It means helping him test a new situation to see how he can use what he already knows. It means opening new opportunities for him, to learn new things and to have new experiences to perfect skills. Volunteering is becoming an avenue out of powerlessness for people who have been under care or handicapped in some way and can learn skills in a less risky situation by volunteering.

We have to recognize that volunteers are motivated because they want to belong to something and that we ought to bring them together and have them feel that they are part of the whole team. Frequently, it may be the most meaningful part of their volunteer experience that they are recognized as part of the team. They seek relationships with a cause. Mental Health care is one of the most important causes in our world today. The groups in the retardation field are largely a voluntary sector made up of consumers, parents of children with special learning needs. They need to be extended by having people who are not consumers, who are volunteers. Speaking out on their behalf because the volunteer can say things that neither the consumer nor the provider of services can say without jeopardizing either his service or his job.

Many people feel powerless in our world today. Volunteering is a way to overcome that feeling and make a big difference. The other aspect of individuals is how they feel, what they like, what they don't like, and what they feel loyal to, who they think they are, whether we're treating them appropriately for who they are. We must consider these in every design that we set up which involves a volunteer, staff member and the patient. This is why volunteer administration is such an important profession. I know that you are glad that the Department of Labor has finally recognized this; the next step is to get Civil Service to make sure that they understand that this is a new profession and that it needs people of tremendous competence in order to connect people to people in meaningful roles. Charles Truax talked about the "helping person" and to me the volunteer is the helping person whom we need in the right spot, where the most important needs are, which best fit the way he feels about his mission and the way we feel about our mission in developing responsive and individualized services to all the people who need our care. Good luck to you as you go on and help in the building of this profession.

22

Volunteer Services Seminar

Ramada Inn, Albany, New York, December 12-13, 1974

Last night we talked about the early leadership of the State Volunteer Services Department, especially developing service opportunities for volunteers, to extend and strengthen what the paid staff does in services for patients and the changing goals for patient care. This morning we're going to be talking less about me and what I do now than about you and what you do and what is expected of you. But it's helpful to know the background from which a speaker comes to you, and what support that means for your work. The Department of Health, Education and Welfare had somebody on volunteers in Manpower and Training, with the Social and Rehabilitation Services, for several years, but that position was pretty limited by the bureaucratic pecking order.

When I tell you that now the job is in the Office of the Secretary, I don't want you to feel that I have coffee with the brass every morning. There are some 2500 other people in the Office of the Secretary! However, it does mean the Office of Volunteer Development cuts across *all* units in HEW, because the need for volunteers in Health and Education, as well as in SRS dealing with rehabilitation and welfare, has been recognized. The position was created within the new office of Human Development. I forecast that soon all programs of HEW will follow the advocacy of the Office of Human Development, in tune with the changing role of the federal government under "new federalism."

*Presented at the Volunteer Services Seminar, Albany New York, December 1974

At this point, legislation is especially important. We all follow news bulletins closely, because often a law can be passed that could turn our jobs upside down. This happened about two weeks ago when the Rehabilitation Act was passed, changing legal concepts of rehabilitation, which tended to be limited to *vocational* rehabilitation. Now, the Rehabilitation Services Administration under the Office of Human Development, will focus on quality of life for *all* citizens, not only the potentially employable. Volunteering can become an important step in rehabilitation for the people possibly leading to employment, but at least improving morale and self-concept.

The Office of Human Development is concerned with special vulnerable groups and their needs. Advocacy for them as persons who are children, youth, aging or in some way disadvantaged, is part of the services of Office of Child Development, the Office of Youth Development, the Administration on Aging. Smaller offices serve Native American Programs, the Handicapped, Rural Americans, consumers of services and veterans.

The Office of Volunteer Development, of all these, is the newest and one of the smallest. We are there as *advocates* for human development as much as any other office, and we consider volunteers to be important humans themselves, but our primary responsibility is to make advocates of volunteers for the vulnerable people with whom they serve. The trend in this direction is greatly acclerated by the "new federalism" in which decision-making powers go to States and to local general purpose governments. The Federal government happens to have the handiest way to raise money, but this does not mean that Washington understands local situations, or can oversee what happens to that money locally. Therefore, responsibility for the distribution of federal monies falls more and more heavily on states and local governments.

We all know the most common mistake in volunteer administration made by newcomers, is getting the volunteers, before you know what you want them to do. I think the same kind of mistake has been made in revenue sharing under the new federalism, in giving the money before the local people are ready to use it. Only 3 percent went for services the first year. Instead of the crucial *people* priorities, here are some examples of what happened:

In the State of New Jersey, three towns have new golf courses. In Pasadena, California, tennis courts were paved and lighted with more than a half million dollars. What people didn't realize was that along with the new federalism had come great pressure for elimination of federal categories of special services. Community Mental Health was one of the major cutback areas.

Ultimately, we will all be looking to state and local government for support for human services, paid for with revenue sharing money. We as volunteer leadership staff must quickly develop an *informed caring citizenry* to influence that decision making. The only requirements in the Local Government Services Act, which authorized revenue sharing monies for the period from '72 through '77, are that there has to be published a Planned Use Report and then there has to be published an Actual Use Report. The Office of Revenue Sharing started to worry about involving citizens when the first Planned Use Reports came in showing less than 3 percent of the monies were being used for intangible human services! Most of the monies went for fire-houses, police departments, bridges and roads. In my own voting and taxpaying town of Clinton in the State of New York, I discovered the federal revenue sharing money all went to road building. Where were the volunteers from the many state programs in Dutchess County when that money all went for roads? They didn't see any connection between what they were doing as volunteers and what was happening to the revenue resources that were being returned to their government to meet the needs for their locality!

Our major responsibility as volunteer administrators is to make sure that our volunteers understand their own powers in local decision-making, and the fact that they *can* turn such priorities around. The difference is that people who want to build buildings, bridges, or Salt Lake City, which built 14 firehouses, the brick and mortar people have a *plan*. They know exactly how much it is going to cost, they know what materials it will require, they know how long it will take to do it, and they can go in and say how this will benefit the town right down to the last penny. Plans are a great relief to local decision makers: they just buy a whole package! So now it has become *our job* to help our volunteers with patients and staff together to put together a plan, estimate what it will cost, help the volunteers take that plan for human services to the budget decision makers! Our patient needs should be among the choices of general purpose governments about where revenue sharing monies are going to go. More and more *is* going for human services in other states. Why not here?

The Office of Human Development is built to focus concern on human beings and human needs. I believe volunteers are natural born advocates for human needs. I believe that volunteering meets a basic human need of everyone, so is a *right* for patients and clients as well as the privileged to be *givers*. To support volunteering is ultimately to strengthen the quality of life in every community. A community can be a ward in a state hospital, or sometimes a community can be a whole metropolitan area around a big city.

Consumers are beginning to recognize that they have legal rights and responsibilities for what they get, and so they are getting into the planning process. The providers have always been in the planning process as paid experts on special disciplines, such as Social Services, Health Educators and so on. Many laws mandate consumer participation. The new Elementary and Secondary Education Act doesn't say a word about volunteers but it says a great deal about parent participation. Parents are consumers. But when providers and consumers come together to set priorities, there is an inevitable difference in perspectives and interests. We volunteer administrators know that volunteers represent a potentially neutral balancing mediating power. They believe in what they know from experience. We all act on the basis of what we believe, which may not happen to be true. Therefore, volunteer training and development means helping volunteers to gain knowledge that is authentic and true, so that they will really understand accurately what is needed. As long as we "use" volunteers for dull limited jobs and don't give them developmental experiences, they're going to believe strange and wonderful myths about what the needs are, because their experience will be too narrow. So we have an obligation to develop a system of volunteer administration which values mobility for volunteers as a means of deepening their understanding. No longer can we brag about a volunteer who's done the same thing for 17 years.

Now new criteria are important to us as administrators: How many aspects of the service do the volunteers understand? How much do volunteers understand about the people being served and what their needs are? How much competency and authenticity has each volunteer gained from being a part of our service delivery pattern? How frequent are reviews of volunteer placements? Mobility, with new training for new responsibilities is the key. Job changes should be horizontal, as well as vertical, not simply being promoted in one service to higher levels, although that's valuable too. But seeing several kinds of treatment activities means gaining understanding of the interrelatedness of human services and needs.

They are not "our" volunteers, but autonomous, free to grow and learn. No one job meets *all* of their needs, so let them move on with our blessing.

A second value of mobility is for program development: the number of outside relationships that a volunteer builds on behalf of our service. We're not losing a volunteer when a volunteer goes into another agency and carries some responsibility for awhile. We're simply sending an ambassador, and that volunteer will return to our service much better informed and with deeper commitment to the needs that we are attempting to meet if he's had that other experience as well.

There has to be some system of showing what volunteers are able to do, and getting their perspective of what's going on into the planning process. We have not involved volunteers enough in planning. Once in awhile we've had a token volunteer on a team, but when the team really got down to the nitty-gritty, the crucial volunteer potential for mediating between conflicting interests often was not realized. Sometimes conflicting interests are professional turfdom, such as between psychologists and psychiatrists. Sometimes mediation is needed between the providers of service and the patients who have not really accepted the same goals for the service, or the plans. The volunteer approaches this as an unpaid, disinterested neutral, no matter how technically qualified he is, with a freedom of perspective which is terribly important. It becomes even more important when he moves out of our service into community planning because he is not perceived as building an empire, which is the accusation leveled at the providers of services and at consumers.

Don't *use* volunteers; that is my plea. Our job is to involve citizens in meeting human needs in the best possible way, in the

services they render whether those services come within our programs or outside. If we do a good leadership job as professional
administrators, volunteers become advocates for our patients
wherever they go. I'm sure that all of us have had a basic fear when
a volunteer resigns: *My* volunteer is leaving! But with experience
we learn that the only way you can really claim people is to free
them. When we clutch volunteers and put a ceiling on what we
allow them to do, we lose three-quarters of the benefit of having
them involved in the service.

Our job as administrators is volunteer *development.* This is not
just the how-to for the entry-level jobs that they do, but it is
developing motivation to improve the service for the patients. Sometimes that can be done from within our program and sometimes
it has to be done from outside. We have to *free* our volunteers if we
really believe in the mission of our services. We have to free our
volunteers to leave us and to speak on behalf of the goals that we
shared, because while they were with us, they made the program
goals their personal goals. They can do a lot more sometimes when
they're outside of our programs than they can inside.

If programs are designed by providers as traditionally they were
for many years, they become programs organized on the basis of
what providers like to do. We social workers may like to do certain
kinds of services or recreationists some kind of special activity.
Therefore, when we develop a program plan, we plan to do what
we like to do, and what we feel we do best. From the consumer
standpoint that may not be meeting *their* needs at all. Everywhere,
consumers are really demanding to be served when they can
articulate this. We have a great many consumers in the mental
health field who cannot speak for themselves, but their families
who do and can are poorly received. They need volunteer mediators
and spokesmen.

We do not have enough people in communities who look at all
the tax monies and all the revenue sharing monies that come into
that community, who also understand the mental health needs of
that community well enough to give it priority in planning the
budget for that community. If we don't ask our volunteers, and
we ourselves simply knuckle under when mental health services
get a very low priority, we're not going to be able to meet the needs

and the goals of our services. We're just going to stop growing. Other people who want those monies are involving people who pick up *their* cause and turning them loose with decision makers. My plea is to see that the citizens who work with us use their tremendous power to make sure that there are services to meet mental health needs in their community.

We hold great human power in our hands as we begin our work with volunteers. But if we don't have a system, a logical sequence of opportunities for volunteers to give them the learning that they need in order to carry this increasingly important responsibility, they will always be service volunteers and never become advocates. They probably won't stay too long even in service roles because it gets mighty dull if you don't think you're getting anywhere.

In the past few years mental health authorities have developed mental health plans. Citizens have not been largely involved though they were invited. I remember going to Governor Rockefeller's "Neighborhood Budget Meeting" here in Albany around 1969-70 when he had one of his annual pilgrimages interpreting his budget. Irving Blumberg who was a paid lobbyist for the State Committee against Mental Illness and for the State Mental Health Association made an impassioned plea for New York State to get out of the costly ski resort business and use the money for state hospital food. He said patients were being fed on a diet which cost 62¢ a day per patient. Now, in today's inflationary terms, that sounds impossible but that was literally true in 1969. And when Irving Blumberg was talking, Governor Rockefeller and his staff were on the podium and you could see a sort of glazed look going over their eyes because they had heard all this before. When Blumberg stopped speaking about 20 hands went up and I thought "Hooray, somebody's going to speak out for the patients in our mental hospitals!" But the first nine speakers were ski operators who also wanted New York State out of the ski business, and who couldn't have cared less about the patients in our mental hospitals. *Not one citizen got up and spoke on behalf of the patients.* I couldn't stand it and I got up and recalled Irving Blumberg's reason for citing the losses from ski resorts. I could see right away I was seen as a paid staff member, empire building if I wanted more budgeted for the Department of Mental Hygiene. There were no citizens there to say "I have worked with the mentally ill and know the needs of people upon discharge from a state hospital; I know we've got to have more adequate provision for these people because I've been there. I didn't get paid to do it, I did it as a volunteer." There was nobody there who could say that. That's when I began to talk about developing citizen advocacy as the volunteer administrator's social role, not to be second-class personnel officers to recruit unpaid labor! For one thing, paid labor isn't going to let that happen in a tight job market. Volunteering is now under justifiable questioning by organized labor. I had an opportunity to take this question to Leo Perlis of the AFL-CIO the other day because I became so much concerned with two things: one was in the State of New York; the New York State Federation of Teachers at State level passed a policy to get all the volunteers out of the public school systems in the State of New York, with Albert Schanker's blessing. I called Henrietta Rabe, whom I had known on the Governor's Interdepartmental Committee for Volunteers, and asked what had happened. It turns out that the *local* teachers' unions did not agree. They didn't adopt the policy adopted at the State level. Could it be because school bond issues are usually successful where there are school volunteers? But there are still volunteers in the public school systems.

The other case has affected mental health. The State of Washington has probably the strongest Governor's Office of Volunteers in the country, of which there are now 24, and none in New York State! That State was negotiating a contract between state employees and the Civil Service Employees Association. A clause was written into that CSEA contract saying that no volunteer may do anything that a paid staff member has ever done. Now there are three state hospitals in the State of Washington with no volunteers and others are considering the same policy. Leo Perlis, a firm believer in volunteerism, sees unionism as volunteerism as Director of Community Services for AFL-CIO. In effect, he said the same thing N.O.W. is saying, "give volunteers the power to improve the system and we'll never have to get rid of them because that's what we are trying to do too." Every local union is autonomous, and actually often every steward is more or less autonomous. Where the steward is *with* the volunteer program, there's been no threat to having volunteers there. Trouble has come where the steward has not been brought into the planning process for having volunteers and for giving them developmental experiences and for selling them on the philosophy of the service.

Another way to bring volunteers into the planning system is to broaden Advisory Committees. That is the basis; that's where you start in developing a system. You don't think it up out of your own head. You convene a group of people who represent *every* point of view in your community and then you plan a voluntary service with connections to the rest of the community. It is not "in-house"; it is a community planning group. And then they develop opportunities for volunteers to be attracted to your program, to make your program goals their personal goals. You help them from the word "go" in the design of your program so that they know when they come in "This is where we're at now, this is where we want to go and we can help shape the future."

People will come and do almost any kind of task if they believe in the goals and they know they're going to make an important difference. Every volunteer needs to understand why we're all trying to improve the services, both in-house and in the community, how to get the other resources that our patients need, and the kinds of community services which may involve no staff at all, self-help kinds of groups. We have an obligation to find volunteer opportunities for our patients in all of these, if their goals are related to what we're trying to do for the people we serve.

Volunteer Administrators don't operate in isolation, we operate as part of a very complex network in the community. And every volunteer comes to us not from his private vacuum, but from a whole network of his own. We've got to get those people who do offer to serve with us to become so inspired with the goals of our service that they become involvers of other people in ever-widening circles in the community about the needs of the people we serve.

Such a system doesn't happen without a great deal of planning, and without a good deal of good hard work. It doesn't have to be done alone. An Advisory Committee is tremendously helpful. Several coordinators operate administratively with groups of task forces who do recruiting, resource mobilization, orientation and training. All the kinds of things that we would do without our office in the beginning can be delegated out to interested volunteers as promotion and recognition for volunteers.

One of the gals who ran a program like that is writing the best book on volunteer management there is—watch for it! It isn't on this bibliography because it isn't due out until January, but Marlene Wilson of Boulder, Colorado has done a book on "The Management of Volunteer Programs." She was able to work one day a week at her office and trust her Task Forces to run that volunteer program four days a week. Now that, to me, is beautiful management, since management is the accomplishment of goals through the efforts of other people. She not only can write about it but she makes it work.

I used to say when I was around (you old-timers will remember) "You shouldn't be in your offices more than 25% of the time." You should be within your facility at least one-quarter of the time looking for new volunteer opportunities and getting a reading on how it's going. You should be at least one-half the time in the community, not just recruiting, but assessing the community level of service for our people, cranking up community people who are equally concerned and turning them loose to innovate in an advocate way.

In order to make this happen in other human services, the Office of Human Development asked me to devise a system. I had to put my whole philosophy of volunteer administration on two pages of paper. I'd like to review it with you because it may take time and I need your thinking. These will be general guidelines, not official regulations, since we are cutting down on red tape. Please help us to make them useful and valid. Nothing happens unless budget people understand what you're doing; and that's just as true for you where you live as it is where I live. But finally they asked me to lay forth the reasons for having a governmental volunteer program, some definitions which would apply generally, and then a system.

I'm going to read some of this to you because every state getting federal monies for programs in the human service areas of health, and that includes mental health, education and welfare will have HEW program evaluators who will look at the state plan to see whether it meets good standards. They will soon have standards for the volunteer components. It could mean a lot of change in the way volunteers are treated in some programs, but it shouldn't surprise any of you who have been around here for very long, because these are the principles on which we based our initial efforts. It starts out, "Not only a staffing resource, volunteers can be ambassadors or advocates for human needs at every level from service delivery to national priority in these days of shrinking budgets. All long-range plans should reflect the necessary explicit administrative provisions for volunteer participation in service and administrative roles to carry out program goals. A sound system is essential to obtain volunteers." It is based on the following principles: "A volunteer is a person who gives gratuitous services" (and that's important, that word "gratuitous" because there is a 1906 federal law forbidding volunteers in federal programs. Later, there was an attorney general's opinion that people can give service to federal offices with a contract in which there's a disclaimer for pay, called "gratuitous service"). Reimbursement of expenses involved as needed is the basic provision for people needing to be enabled to be volunteers. It is not payment for service.

Second: A volunteer supplements but does not supplant paid staff, working in concert toward shared objectives on individual or group assignments.

Third: Volunteering, a basic right, is essential human developmental experience for all persons; a means for learning, developing wholesome relationships, and contributing to the quality of life. Volunteer opportunities should be provided for all persons. This means patients and residents as well as other persons, particularly the members of vulnerable groups we serve. Everyone can help someone.

Fourth: Freedom of choice, which is essential to the volunteer, is equally important to the staff involved and to the person being served. (In other words, you don't place a volunteer with an unwilling staff member or with an unwilling consumer of services.) But that freedom carries responsibility best defined in clear, contractual terms.

Fifth: Volunteers work with, and not for, other people. Mobility and progression for volunteers are dynamic values to all the persons involved in matching interests and needs in order to realize more fully the human development potential. Volunteer assignments should be subject to periodic review, evaluation with, by and of volunteers. And those services range from prevention to rehabilitative objectives.

Sixth: Evaluation of volunteer participation means assessing the impact of the service on the recipient. What difference does it make to have the volunteer there? It means assessing the impact of the service on the paid staff work, on the agency as a whole, and on the volunteer himself. (In other words, there are four components in evaluation of volunteer services and hardly any of them have anything to do with numbers!) Since most people have a basic rescue fantasy, assessment of impact is essential to show volunteers, staff, recipients and administrators the effectiveness of the service. Quantification should reflect numbers of volunteers, nature of services, extent of target population served. Impact should be expressed in human benefit terms such as institutionalization, or recidivism, prevented, capacities built and signs of development in the people involved, the consumer, volunteer and the staff members involved.

A cost/benefit ratio must be amplified by an analysis of these intangibles to be meaningful.

A volunteer system starts small and involves building a climate in which people will risk giving their best. An ideal program is staffed with a full-time administrator, who decentralizes his administration to line staff as readiness is indicated. Client volunteering is now established as a route out of powerlessness. Provision of opportunity to participate in policy development and advocacy roles are elements in the experience which attracts and motivates the best volunteers. On those principles, we've divided the process into three stages: preparation, operation, and evaluation.

Under preparation, we have divided the responsibility between the executive, the volunteer director or coordinator, and the line staff or supervisor of volunteers. And there's a function for each of them in having a volunteer program. The executive must clarify the goals for the total program for the paid staff work. He must suggest objectives for volunteer participation, which may include program enrichment, outreach and extension, that old multiplier factor. (I often cite Mt. McGregor School where a speech therapist said to me, "If I were here alone, I could serve 15 residents; with 50 Skidmore college girls, I serve 400." This is the kind of cost/benefit that has meaning to budgeteers and it's the kind of language we have to be able to speak, even in the preparation stage.) Interpretation—this is the executive or his ambassador in the community, mobilizing support and setting standards and norms. The volunteers have a responsibility in setting standards and norms and they can say things that we can't say as staff members in the preparation stages.

I'm suggesting that ideally we need a full-time qualified director to focus all efforts and we need the executive to designate staff time for work analysis, to define roles, and prepare training. We need communication from the top through staff meetings and memos of authorization. The volunteer director, then, having come in very early, has to work on defining goals and objectives for the volunteer services to work with administrative authorities, unit heads, line staff, representative volunteers and consumers, defining the needs for volunteers. And so it goes on down the line. The line staff has to look at their own work, and to say what is appropriate for volunteers in their service. We have to have these three responsibilities carried by these three kinds of people before we get the first volunteer, because we've got to know what we need volunteers to do before we ask them to come. Gone are the days when we can say "come one, come all." We've got to plan all of recruiting and training and recognition based on such preparation work.

Now you say, "What do I do? I came in when we were long past the preparation stages." I guess my message to you this morning is: if it hasn't been done, that's where you'd better put your own priorities first. Because if it isn't done, you're going to find in your communities people that don't believe in the objectives of the Department of Mental Hygiene. They've been burned. Their good intentions were not appreciated, or they have not had a good volunteer experience and they are not silent about it. They're saying that the Department of Mental Hygiene doesn't know what it's doing. And all the fancy PR in the world isn't going to meet that kind of doubt in a community program. Public relations and volunteer services have to work hand in glove, or each can undo the other. That's why this system is so terribly important.

In the operations stage, I think the executive has continuing monitoring and support responsibility for everything that goes on. The executive communicates the reward system in the organization.

We hope it doesn't reward the people that keep volunteers out, but rewards the people who work well with volunteers, which is easier said than done. Probably, it's far more comfortable temporarily for an administrator to have nobody rocking the boat. Most find it pays off to be conscientious and are secure enough to have people come and see what's going on, to welcome the idea of amplifying services and developing community understanding of the program objectives through volunteer involvement. One thing we can say to administrators is "If you don't have volunteers who talk enthusiastically about your program, how do you get your message out? What does the public perceive behind those walls? Why do you have budget problems? Don't you need somebody to help?"

The volunteer director has to take responsibility to focus efforts on targeted recruiting, knowing the kinds of people needed to do the things that need to be done, and going after those people. A competent volunteer administrator shifts operations onto other shoulders soon, making the operations phase an organizing, delegating and monitoring function in the operating stages. For each of you, it means don't do it yourself. It means working through the efforts of other people, giving appropriate learning opportunities for people as they need them, including for the line staff on how to work with volunteers. Then the line staff becomes part of the total effort in developing volunteers, because they have *their* volunteers, no longer *your* volunteers. Everyone gets to see the value of mobility and progression and advocacy roles for volunteers, each for his own interests. Line staff come to understand that it's not safer to try to do it alone; it takes teamwork, citizen volunteers have become advocates for their team mates.

The only way we're going to have human needs met is to have more people who care involved in effort to meet them. The more informed and frustrated volunteers become about unmet needs, the more power they muster in the community. They will exercise this citizen power in an adversary stance if they have not been brought into the team. But they will exercise it as representatives of the team when they are also providers of services, *on behalf of the program,* and become the best ambassadors and community mobilizers we could have.

In the evaluation stage, I think there are equal divisions of responsibilities between the executive, the volunteer director, and the unit staff. And every one of them should involve volunteers and consumers when they are looking back at what has been going on, deciding what the new needs are. This starts the whole preparation operations cycle over again.

In many ways, all this depends on the self-concept and the vision of the volunteer coordinator. The volunteer coordinator who takes this as just a job, who's willing to sit in the office and wait for people to ask for volunteers and to wait for volunteers to come in and offer their services is going to contribute very little to the meeting of human needs.

This is an action-oriented, professional responsibility, not miscellaneous clerical work, as the 1970 Census called it. It involves faith in people and trust in volunteers. It involves some of the skills and characteristics of all the helping professions. You've heard me talk about the Truax Triad, but let's look again at integrity—genuineness, accurate empathy, and non-possessive warmth. I really hear you, and I'm with you. I don't get my kicks from having you depend on me. I get my kicks in seeing your growing independence and our interrelationship, each with an appropriate role. And then I go back to the doctor who was setting up the South Shore Mental Health Center who said to me about these qualifications, "There's another very important one you'd better get in there: a high tolerance for ambiguity and confusion." You can't live in this volunteer world if you have to have things in neat packages. Most of all, what I want to say to you is: With your great privilege of taking the offer of service from the public and applying it in your programs comes the commensurate responsibility of giving those persons a good developmental experience for their own personal needs and for the needs of your service.

The word responsibility means "response." It means being able to respond and not so wedded to a system and so inflexible that you can only respond on Mondays to Fridays from 9:00 a.m. to 5:00 p.m. It means being able to readjust to meet the offer of service with appreciation that's meaningful, not token. It means evaluation which really looks at what happens to all the people involved, facing up to what was good and what wasn't good. That's why you need your own personal value system about what's most important

in this world and what's good. We need a profession. I think we're a
long way from having one, and I'm having some second thoughts
about going too fast on this professionalizing bit. I'm a social
worker at heart, and to me when social work became a profession,
it began to lose the idealism that had motivated a lot of us to join.
It's the same rescue fantasy that I talked about with volunteers,
and it became so systematized and so self-centered rather than
other-centered that it has lost a great deal of power. To me a profession is made up of a group of trustworthy people who commit
themselves to responsibility because they have ability and the open
learning attitude to improve their own competency, and who
share their leadership and to develop the fullest human capacities
in other people. I think that is what we're talking about when
we're talking about taking responsibility for volunteers in today's
world, and enjoying the privilege of working with man at his best.

23

Impact of Volunteering on the Health Field

Meanings and values are changing. Health is no longer just the absence of illness, according to the World Health Organization, but physical, social, psychological and mental well-being; a right, no longer the privilege of a lucky few. Prevention, most appealing to volunteer idealism, includes not only prophylactic activities, but nutrition, parenthood education, decent housing—the whole gamut of "general welfare" in the Preamble to the Constitution. Treatment is intervention to ease the crisis and begin rehabilitation immediately, to prevent permanent damage or chronicity. Throughout this continuum of services, volunteers reinforce and extend the effectiveness of paid staff, however they are credentialed and add a morale factor which motivates patients to make the best possible use of available services. Volunteers multiply the capabilities of agencies to carry out their missions from before birth to dying, throughout the life span. They bridge people from one service to another, and they offer continuity of caring for a person as he begins to manage on his own, to build social supports which will help him toward economic independence, self-confidence and enjoyment of his other relationships. Rather than a "job", some volunteers and recipients prefer assignment of person to person, with their joint activities determining the nature of the tasks involved in a succession of situations. Volunteers represent the connective tissue in our society, and some of us believe they may well be preventing its total disintegration.

Presented at the Association of Volunteer Bureaus Jubilee Kansas City Mo. May 1976.

Volunteer administration makes a big difference. Skills in matching people to people include leadership development, organization of groups for continuous learning and feedback loops from volunteers to contribute to the program as a whole, influence policies and innovate activities. Since health services used to rest entirely on the authority of "Doctor's Orders", it is a struggle to free both staff and volunteers to speak up, dream up and stir up establishment patterns combining basic humane values with expert technology and skills. Leadership to focus many perspectives on a shared goal comes from people who think in humane terms, not diagnostic labels. Volunteers have objectives like those of their partners on the paid staff when they are nurtured through a progression of learning opportunities, on a variety of assignments, with appreciative recognition along the way. Probably the health field has realized less of the individual volunteer's ability than other settings, less rigid than hospitals. Recently there are signs of more trust, and more latitude for health volunteers because of more professional volunteer administrations, and more mobility among services for volunteers.

Such leadership produces the kind of informed citizenship which is now needed in Health Planning and Resource Development, as mandated by that 1974 law (P.L. 93-641). The required governing body of 10 to 30 members must be broadly representative of the social, linguistic and racial populations, major purchasers of health care, geographically selected from the health service area, a majority consumers with no financial interest in the provision of health care. P.L. 93-154, Emergency Medical Services Systems, has a similar provision. If the proposed block grants for health also become law, there will be opportunities at every governmental level for citizen participation in planning and prioritizing resources for health purposes. Who those non-provider citizens are is very important to the quality of life in every community.

Every volunteer comes with a different perspective, and a different potential. In the past there was no way to get volunteer suggestions into the hopper. Now there are many in welfare, under Title XX, of the Social Security Act, as in housing, in education, community services and economic development, aging, all kinds of developmental disability services—all these fields now have provisions for citizen input. Cynically, we can rest assured that financial interests will be represented, and, increasingly, consumers will be there. The danger is that these two, eyeing one another with suspicion, at risk in the decision-making process, will not come to a sound consensus. Experience with General Revenue Sharing shows that funds which are not designated specifically tend to go for hardware, not human services. Hardware seems to be visible, tangible evidence—a monument for posterity to the priorities that now exist.

Volunteers do turn resources toward people priorities when they realize how authentic is their first-hand observation, how practical are their opinions, how right they can be about how things ought to be, and most of all, how much impact they could have! They have built most of the hospitals—now they must turn their energies to building *services* where and when they are needed.

The Congress has pointed the way, even overriding veto on Health Revenue Sharing and Health Act, and the Public Health Service Amendments are other mandates for majority non-providers on advisory committees. If volunteers continue in palliative service roles when they could improve public policies for health, they are contributing to serious geographic injustices particularly to those in rural and inner city areas who are least well served. Just be sure to have *your* heart attack where good medical services are easily accessible!

Volunteers pioneered health services because of their compassionate response to persons in distress. However, as in other fields, as health services have become institutionalized, the volunteer has been displaced by paid, formally trained staff in direct service roles. Relegated to supportive, interpretive and indirect services, as medical technology became more complex (and expensive) the volunteer has seen the gap between the ideal and the actual care of most people widen. Consumers of health services are less willing to remain unserved, or poorly served, and their needs are being expressed even in malpractice suits. Health differs from other fields of human services because sooner or later everyone is a "consumer".

Quotations of the numbers of volunteers and the monetary value of their hours of service vary tremendously. In 1974, AHA estimated 1,800,000 auxilians of whom 500,000 were service volunteers. The auxiliaries raised $54 million for hospitals. More importantly, careful analysis of the impact of volunteering on the patient, the staff, the outreach of services and the quality of experiences people have, is beginning to interest scholars and practitioners of the art of volunteer administration. Evaluation is now an essential part of the planning, operation and program cycle, but in these times of shifting values, we have not articulated explicitly the good and worthwhile and important except in such quantified terms, which do not tell the whole story. To convince the people who control the purse strings, we have blithely claimed that volunteers enrich services in ways not otherwise (budgetwise!) possible, that they have relationships with people which are somehow different from purchased services, that their humane viewpoint prevents the technology from becoming more important than the person. We believe these truths to be self-evident, but in these days of cost-benefit accountability, we are going to have to invent new systems which cost less, without sacrificing these essential values.

Secretary Matthews recently described a health shopping center (community multi-service center) where services averaged $33.00 as opposed to $215 a day in the nearest hospital. How would you like that for your town? What can you and volunteers do? He suggests that teachers, agricultural agents, many other people could have roles in improving health, deinstitutionalization of services, increasing individual responsibility for consequences of unhealthy behavior such as smoking, pollution, etc. Think what could be changed if everyone volunteered to help.

Volunteer impact is most appreciated now for the easing of institutional strictures and the stigma ignorance attached to many diseases years ago. But the tragedy today is how few persons are getting the best health care possible: those near great medical centers or with the most interesting cases. As volunteers assume responsibility for planning on decision-making bodies they interpret needs from first hand observation to providers of services. They explain services to consumers in language they can understand and extend the outreach, facilitate schedules and delivery "receiving systems" to fit local cultural patients. Call it humanizing, or deinstitutionalizing, the volunteer is protection from rules made for the convenience of staff. He is going to bat for the patient, his family, his dignity and worth as a person, in an ombudsman process. With access to power centers in the community he needs facts like these:

Health costs advanced 14% the first quarter of this year while the Cost of Living Index rose 2.4%. Hospital service charges increased 20.1%, according to a study by the Council on Wage and Price Stability. Alternatives to present patterns of care must be found. Adequate care has become a luxury, and real prevention seems an impossible dream. People are unaware of what they might have because *they* don't decide what to get: doctors or legislators do. The National Institute on Alcohol Abuse and Alcoholism estimates that more than 9 million Americans have drinking problems, 100,000 new cases a year and more than 25,000 auto deaths yearly are involving alcohol. A dozen countries have lower infant mortality rates than ours. For men, thirty other countries have longer life expectancy rates than we do.

There are organizations to attack almost every disease known to man. The role of the volunteer sector has traditionally been out front to show the way, and in many fields this is still true. As the chief source of research funds, however, the government plays an important role. The partnership with voluntary agencies and those of paid staff with volunteers which should always exist are needed now more than ever.

24

The Service Agency Looks at Student Volunteers

Swamped in October, bone dry by Christmas, the agency manpower planner regards student volunteers as a mixed blessing. Hard pressed for funds, each agency has to justify taking on any kind of new staff in cost/benefit terms. Twenty hours of service of which five are spent in training (which also ties up expensive staff time) produce an equation dangerously close to no margin of benefit. Some agencies aren't very enthusiastic about any volunteers, and students seem to them to be more likely to rock the boat than others, asking questions which have no easy answers. Fortunately, a few agencies see the benefits which are there.

In the face of such negative attitudes, it is remarkable that student volunteering has burgeoned into one of the largest categories of persons serving in many agencies, and that colleges and schools seeking placements for field experience are able to find them. Agencies feel student programs are a luxury to them. Unfortunately, in some communities, students simply shop around with little campus guidance until they find a place to put in their hours. If they are lucky, they find a volunteer director who can counsel them into a spot where they can have a valid learning experience, do something worthwhile and explore vocational choices through firsthand observation and contact. In others, they are perceived as free labor and put to work doing tasks the staff dislikes to do. So they leave.

Agency orientation and training are essential to volunteer effectiveness. No matter how sophisticated and knowledgeable any new staff member is, orientation, developing a new identity, with new relationships, accepting and internalizing specific new goals and objectives, is essential for fitting into a new role in a new setting, and working there with volunteers is part of the adjustment. Training becomes a process for testing personal goals for congruence with those of the other persons with whom one works: the "consumer" of volunteer services, and the other paid providers of agency services, as well as the volunteers. Most agencies have found the best way to develop teamwork is to begin in orientation and training.

Promotion from direct service to policy and program development roles for staff and volunteers is an opportunity particularly significant for students. Their idealism and fresh viewpoint is a priceless contribution to the planning process. Volunteering experience can qualify them for positions on policy making levels, within agencies, and in community groups. Under the new federalism, many laws are thrusting decision-making about priorities for limited community resources, revenue sharing and United Fund disbursement back to the community level. The informed citizenry which this trend requires should include student volunteers with fresh knowledge of current theory and keen observation. Slowly it is dawning on communities that the old "easy money" days of federal categorical programs are over, and that the money distributed under General and Special Revenue Sharing and block grants is subject to many competing demands in every community. Expectations whetted by experimental and demonstration short term projects are building constituencies which feel the worth of the initial experiment proves their need and ought to justify high priority. Students are less awed by traditional hierarchies, and are ardent advocates for what they believe to be just.

At the same time, they need to learn some grim realities, that there are real limits to local and federal resources, especially during the current "stagflation" high unemployment and depression. Bricks and mortar are wearing out, and demands for services ever increasing. Nowhere better than at public hearings can students see the real taxpayer rebellion and the intensified competition for support of human services.

As the power structure decision-makers of tomorrow, students need maximum exposure to all facets of human needs, all forms of services and all means of problem solving. The current college generation will be the responsible work force supporting services for an ever-increasing proportion of elderly persons, who have organized effectively and vote according to responsiveness to their needs. (Appropriations for programs for the Older Americans often exceed the estimates submitted by the bureaus responsible for implementing them!) School bond issues and budgets are meeting increasing resistance, with falling enrollments. A few years ago, it was said to be the other way around; schools and children took top priority, but this seems no longer to be true. Student group activism has calmed down as advocacy for other people. A less altruistic activism is emerging in protest to their own tuition costs, which have certainly skyrocketed. They need to see the larger picture, too.

The agencies would like to see a return of some of the altruism which characterized student activists in the 60's and early 70's. Directors of volunteer services are recruiting on a different rationale: no longer "what you can do to change the system", but "how you can acquire qualifying experience as a volunteer for your future career." Many students who have a good experience as volunteers are ultimately hired by the same agency upon graduation. Even if this doesn't work out, the agency finds the ex-volunteer can be interpreter of its program, sympathetic to the needs of its target group.

We have learned in a few years of growing emphasis on field experience education that having students join a staff brings word of new technology or theory which the service professionals might be too busy to learn about, otherwise. The opportunity for direct application and testing is stimulating much needed research in the voluntary sector, and the opportunity for classroom analysis may well improve agency practice. Field experience quality depends on two key counsellors: the quality of the campus counselling which guides student interests to an appropriate agency and the quality of agency counselling and training which reduces the pre-service period and deepens the commitment of the student to the service. Optimum cross fertilization is possible when faculty assist in training agency staff and volunteers, not abdicating the educative function entirely to the agency. Volunteers and agency staff feel truly recognized when asked to teach at a college. We need more of this exchange of wisdom learned from study and wisdom learned from direct observation and personal experience.

We have also learned that group placements double commitment to serve, by adding peer pressure. A volunteer serving with a group has to answer to his peers as well as to the "voluntee" and the paid staff involved. Even if the student volunteer works one-to-one with a client or on his own, his identity as a group member for feedback or social purposes will insure his performance for the honor of the group as well as for the sake of the service. He may want to outshine his fellow group members. Competitiveness is a value as long as it improves performance and reliability and doesn't put stress on the clients involved. The agency has primary accountability for continuity and quality of services, and must monitor paid staff and volunteer service accordingly.

Students are quick to criticize the way people have to diagnose their own problems, and figure out for themselves where to go for help in many communities. Not enough agencies have outreach programs, or reschedule for their constituency needs instead of staff convenience. Students have observed that some agencies are preoccupied with selection of clients to serve, rather than inclusive. Students say they like telephone crisis or information service because there they can offer a meaningful response to urgent needs. The ombudsman is a popular role for students, who need to understand that *class advocacy, for all* the victims of a problem, is much more effective than going to bat for *one* person. Securing preferential treatment for one person may mean real injustices to others quite as needful. Students enjoy being a linking volunteer, as helping a patient in the transition from a mental institution into public school. Such linking gives the only continuous relationship the youth has, and sustains him over a difficult transition period. Agencies cannot afford enough paid staff time to soften the cultural shock as much as volunteers can do.

Alvin Toffler, of *Future Shock* fame, in *Ecospasm* speaks of futurism as "anticipatory participation." It is to be hoped that student volunteers can use field experience learning to improve future human services. The optimism characteristic of youth is greatly needed by social agencies discouraged by fiscal and program demand pressures. Not knowing what has failed in the past, students often go ahead with an idea and prove that it can be done, after all. Often they wind up very respectful of the skills of the staff, and enter the same profession.

Students represent the most rapidly growing category of volunteers. Many helping professions regard student volunteering as upstream recruiting to their calling.

The degree of faculty interest in the agency, willingness to help with orientation, training and follow through with the students is a determinant of how agency staff regard student programs. Students can bridge not only clients but their educational institutions to agencies. Where faculty is indifferent, often agency staff have to be convinced that student volunteers are worth the trouble. Here the agency executive attitude and the reward system of the organization are crucial factors. Paid staff are quick to perceive whether student volunteers are really welcome, and act accordingly. The students win acceptance with responsible, mature behavior and that in itself is a good educational experience!

25

Strengthening Voluntarism From the Public Sector

Just as it seems contradictory to have government strenthening voluntarism, probably no field of human endeavor has more ambiguity of definitions and confusion about meanings than voluntarism. In 1969 I had published a small pamphlet which muddies the waters considerably because I thought I was coining the word *volunteerism* to add to *voluntarism* and *voluntary* which are legitimate words.

The double E stresses the importance of the individual's experience when he freely chooses to offer his time and talents to help someone. That person, the volunteer, has remained the center of my interest consistently, whether I happen to be working in the private sector, where most recently I was accountable to your next speaker, Dr. Robert E. Hill at the National Center for Voluntary Action, on in the largest governmental department in the world, the U.S. Department of Health, Education, and Welfare, where I am now a bureaucrat.

First, I should like to point out that there *is* considerable communication and collaboration, and the trend is toward more cooperating effort between the private and public sectors. A good deal of overlap occurs when a voluntary sector agency becomes supported by grants or purchase of service contracts on a fee or block grant basis, each device using taxpayers' dollars. I applaud this "adhocracy" and only plead for more and better coordination and open communication. Another area of ambiguity exists within the public sector in the varying concepts of the words "volunteers" and

Presented at a National Council on Philanthropy Conference, December 4, 1975 "voluntary" services sometimes within the same law, such as the Social Security Act as amended in 1974. Left over from the Harris Amendments of 1967 is the mandate to the states for the "use and training" of subprofessionals and "nonpaid or partially paid volunteers" in social services and assisting advisory committees for Guam, Puerto Rico and the Virgin Islands. Title I - Social Services for Aging and Medical Assistance for the Aging, Title V - Maternal and Child Health and Crippled Children's Services, Title X - Services to the Blind, Title XIII - Child Welfare Services, XIV - Services to the Permanently and Totally Disabled, Title XVI - Supplemental Security Income for those Blind, Aged or Disabled and Title XIX Medical Assistance. However, Title XX, signed last January, removed the mandate from Title IV A and repealed Title VI, substituting an organization structure requirement that a state's social service plan must show how "public and private agencies and volunteers" will participate in the delivery of services.

The Voluntary Service Act of 1973 legitimizing ACTION was the coalescence of a variety of governmental efforts to promote voluntarism which was promised in the Presidential Inaugural Address of January 20, 1969. The first step was the Cabinet Committee on Voluntary Action which George Romney headed, and appropriately housed an Office of Voluntary Action in HUD. In Febuary 1970, a voluntary sector wing, the National Center for Voluntary Action was formed. The evaluation of governmental efforts included some support from HEW, exemplified by a pamphlet entitled "Small, Splendid Efforts in Voluntary Action" which brought me quickly to Washington to protest that voluntarism deserved more credit than that! Small, Splendid Efforts, indeed!

Actually, there were Citizens Participation units in the Office of Education and in the National Institute of Mental Health, and a staff advisor in Social and Rehabilitation Services for brief periods. Now my office is located in the center for advocacy for vulnerable persons, the Office of Human Development in the Office of the Secretary. In good company, I share information and support the efforts of my staff neighbors who deal with Consumer Involvement, and Manpower and Office of Veterans Affairs as well as the larger units for children, youth, aging and rehabilitation services. We often note that their clientele and mine overlap when volunteering is used as an avenue toward employment, as experiential learning and self testing, and as access to program planning and evaluation for those who have experienced the difficulties which our programs are being designed to alleviate.

But as it has so often been said by George Romney, "Government cannot do the job alone." A democratic society needs voluntarism to be healthy just as the individual needs a chance to give as well as to receive, and, most importantly, all of us need a voice in what happens to us, whether we participate as a provider of services or as a recipient. Noone knows what I want and need better than I do myself, and my neighbors who know me, who know what our community offers, and who have some very good ideas about how it could be improved. Unfortunately, money in the private sector is raised the easiest way, from the people finding it hardest to pay, through payroll deductions. Decisions are not made on what the beneficiary wants, but the wishes of the powerful people who *control* payrolls. The payers carries the heaviest tax load, proportionately, too.

This brought on the rationale underlying the New Federalism which has been an accelerating expression of congressional determination to decentralize decision-making to the state and local governing bodies. The epitome of New Federalism is General Revenue Sharing, which this Administration has stated it will support for renewal for 1977. Actually, the first few years of operation, very little federal revenue shared with states and 38,000 smaller governments *went* to human services: less than 3% in the first year ending in 1973. But gradually the proportion for services rather than for things has been rising, partly because citizens have become involved in setting priorities. During the same period, the Congress was increasingly disenchanted with assistance by categorical grants with all of the red tape and centralized accountability which categories require.

We are seeing a reversal in accountability in this country from upward to the federal government to outward to the voters. Not all of us as private citizens are prepared for the decision-making opportunities we could use. Volunteering is one of the best ways to find out what's going on:

Where the gaps and duplication are, and what are the emerging needs in a shifting economy where services are becoming more usual occupations than manufacturing or farming.

In addition to general revenue sharing, New Federalism meant support for urban development, rural development, manpower development (now under CETA, the Comprehensive Employment and Training Act. Several counties and at least one Governor's Office have used CETA funds to pay for volunteer administration through local Voluntary Action Centers. Other "users" of volunteers include government departments of welfare, law enforcement systems, school systems, museums, civic, drama, music and arts groups.

These developments have highlighted the importance of sound volunteer administration. Varied as these work settings may be, there are ideal basic practices for analysing what needs to be done and dividing the responsibility between paid staff and volunteers, just as we divide the larger assignments between public and private agencies under Title XX, otherwise known as the Social Services Act of 1974. Congress set a 2.5 billion ceiling on moneys for social services, but carefully excluded training for service providers, both staff and volunteer, from that limit. Training is a crucial part of keeping volunteers involved. And it is keeping volunteers, not *recruiting* them, which is the hard part of volunteer administration.

The HEW Office of Volunteer Development is working on a generic Volunteer Development System, applicable in all kinds of settings, in order to strengthen the voluntarism. Not too different from employee turnover figures, volunteers do most of their dropping out early, usually in their first year. Much volunteer dropout could be avoided. But where a volunteer drops out—or, what is even more likely, he is dropped inadvertently by an unprepared agency he is a walking, talking witness to the failure of that agency to deserve support. One large national user of volunteers has acknowledged losing 40,000 volunteers every year. Think of it! Forty thousand negative press agents loose on communities across the land! No wonder you who are concerned with philanthropy and fundraising are having a hard time!

Fortunately, that agency is exceptionally forthright in facing and doing something to correct this problem. Their first step is to improve the paid staffing leadership for volunteers. We hope that our HEW Volunteer Development System will help them and all kinds of agencies to examine their volunteer experiences and to employ competent full time professional level leadership. The first task, more realistically, is to create a new climate of warmth and mutually satisfying respect for the time and effort of both volunteers and staff, so people will stay around long enough to progress to important leadership positions. Leadership of the highest calibre constantly refreshed by continuing learning opportunities, is needed to face the complexities and scope of problems in the Bicentennial year as contrasted with our beginnings. A volunteer development system must become an integral part of the total service system, from the inception of new ideas, to changing policies and practices while operating a program, evaluating realistically all along the way. Volunteers are free of job risk, unlike the paid staff, and free from jeopardizing their access to services they need unlike the consumers. So they become a major resource for the planning process, too. Much new legislation mandates citizen participation in planning. The American Revolution Bicentennial Administration has funded with the Kettering Foundation and twenty-four women's organizations a project of Community Resource Centers which are local self-help groups attacking local problems. This sort of government/voluntary partnership in support of local effort is typical of today's trend in voluntarism.

Since there is no one here to speak about ACTION, and that's one volunteer organization which is not taxing but is reinforcing philanthropic resources, I feel an imperative to clarify that agency's relationship to HEW, and to the voluntary sector. Firstly, and perhaps too simplistically, may I say I regard ACTION as I do NCVA, as coworkers in the vineyard of supporting volunteering. In that sense, those two agencies, governmental and voluntary respectively, are producers of volunteers. In addition to Peace Corps, VISTA, Older Americans, and the student programs, ACTION has fostered the development of mini projects with minigrants, of local services on a project basis, and of statewide programs through seed money for Governors' Offices of Voluntary Action. All have generated a great deal of volunteering for all human services. HEW generates some volunteers, too, because we are stressing the importance of *being* a volunteer for human development, and we are urging programs which ameliorate serious problems to involve victims of those problems as volunteers in designing effective services and delivery systems. But at HEW we are constrained by federal law from having any volunteers working within our offices (U.S. Code 31, Sec. 665b). But most of the programs we are responsible to implement can use volunteer talents to extend and reinforce the paid staff at state and local levels. So, in that light, we are consumers of volunteers—not only the ones ACTION recruits and trains, or NCVA and its local affiliated Voluntary Action Centers refer, but also the ones we generate ourselves. Nothing helps the self-image of a person more than being a successful volunteer, sure that what he is doing is important and needed. Social scientists tell us that low self esteem is the root of many social problems as well as individual anti-social and self-destructive behavior at all socio-economic levels. Volunteering as self-transcendence is an antidote. We are convinced it is a right, not a privilege, because it meets a univeral human need.

Much legislation has been proposed to encourage volunteering through tax benefits, both deductions and credits, but none has become law. The volunteers have not given these priority. The laws we have encourage service volunteering in health planning and resource development, public health facilities, public school parent advisory committees, rehabilitation, community development, veteran's administration hospitals, community services, Native American programs, Head Start, Child Abuse Protection and Prevention, Runaway programs—even the Congressional Budget and Impoundment Control Act—all of the nutrition and planning services for the aged—the list is a long one! Volunteering is encouraged by Civil Service as qualifying persons for admission to examination, if it is well documented as relevant and authentic. Citizens are urged to serve on dozens of kinds of advisory committees. Out of pocket expenses reimbursement and per diem payment are authorized for most of these and staff and administrative support is increasing. The Department of Labor has recognized volunteer administration as professional, not merely clerical work.

The volunteer, who gives his free time for free, costs an investment in staff time for orientation, training, advice and support. That staff is key to volunteer retention as Ann Richardson and Lenore Romney have been testifying from their own experience in volunteering. Government volunteering offers training ground for an informed citizenry, and positions of considerable influence or public policy as rewards. But the investment in staff support pays off as a multiplier of services rendered which no budget could provide, in mobilized community sympathy and support for good services, and ambassadors of good will, facilitating receiving systems for services to complement the delivery systems devised by the experts. The individual volunteer becomes a leader for organized voluntarism who is moved by compassion, educated by experience and capable of preserving the life blood of a pluralistic democratic society. And government is finally beginning to realize how valuable he is!

The government is firmly committed to strengthening voluntarism through stipending volunteers in ACTION, out-of-pocket and administrative costs in the Social Security Act as amended last year. The major difference at HEW is the perception of volunteering as a step into the mainstream, toward employment, as well as an expression of natural human compassion. We are now charged with a systematic progression of volunteers into public policy making positions to plan for more effective services, freely mobile back and forth from govermental to voluntary organizations.

26

The Volunteer and the Volunteer Director in Thanatology

Even the government is fostering volunteering because volunteering is a natural human response to the needs of other persons. In today's society, families are widely scattered, remaining together temporarily in highly mobile nuclear units during the period which children are dependent. Many of the functions which used to be carried by collateral relatives or long term neighbors are now institutionalized or carried by volunteers. Motivated by a critical need, or stress, or their own needs for meaningful relationships, they carry out services which in earlier generations were done within the extended families and neighborhoods, rooted to the home base.

Now, more than one fourth of all Americans volunteer. The entire socio-economic range is represented within their ranks, and nearly all ages. The volunteer of the year award in West Virginia last year went to an 18-month-old AFDC child who with her mother visited elderly people living alone. The popularity of volunteering among the elderly continues to grow, with high school and college students a close second. For both of those groups, volunteering offers a significant identity during a life period when an occupational identity is not available. Volunteering is being regarded as an important developmental experience for persons, a right which more and more people are claiming. The desolate anomie felt by

Presented at an Institute on Volunteers in Thanatology, November 7, 1975 persons dying in some sterile, medical institutions, according to a recent census bureau report,[1] and by their families and survivors, adds another source of anguish and frustration when there is no one around who seems to have time to pay enough attention. Time is allotted to all of us each day in equal amounts, but somehow paid staff never seem to have enough of it. A troubled person hesitates to impinge on the time of busy medical staff, or apartment neighbors whom one doesn't know very well. However, time is the unique factor every volunteer chooses to give. That can mean time by persons facing their own or a relative's death. In other relationships, even if friends and relatives are deeply concerned, their own feelings make listening particularly difficult. What they hear compounds their own grief unbearably.

One of the most cynical critics of volunteering has referred to it as a "compassion trap", stating that service is not worth doing unless it is intended to change the system or is paid for.[2] Perhaps volunteers *can* change our system of dying which would be good, but those who attempt to help people through the loss of their own or a near relative's dying are *feeling with* those people. That is their very reason for being there at that time and afterward. Compassion is an essential humane value, and the means for expressing it are few and inadequate. Volunteering has become a major way to express caring in a materialistic world.

Volunteers in Thanatology help people singly, and in groups. One of the most rapidly growing groups calls itself "The Compassionate Friends" and is made up of parents who have lost a child now reaching out to newly bereaved parents. You will be hearing directly from them here. They, and I agree with them, feel that compassion is a desperately needed emotion in this depersonalized world, and its benefits can never be measured in dollars.

Widow-to-widow groups illustrate another outreach program by victims to more recent victims of tragedy. When one has been helped, she seldom feels she can repay the helper adequately. She then must turn to others with similar needs and pass along the kind of understanding and concern which meant so much to her when she needed it. There is authenticity in the empathy which comes from a person who has undergone the same kind of experience, a ring of insightful sympathy which other people don't have. And it is a way to "repay" the obligation one feels for help which was really helpful. Sometimes a volunteer acts in a helpful way he would have appreciated but did not experience—something he missed when he was in the same spot. Or he may imitate the effective helpers he did know then. In either case, there is a bond in common human experience which binds us humans together. The widows to widows meet in groups with a high turnover because people "graduate" when they no longer need that sustenance. A dropout is often a sign of adjustment to a new life style. "In 1970 there were approximately 12 million widowed persons in this country of whom 10 million or 85% were women."[3]

The American Association of Retired Persons and Retired Teachers Association has a special widowed Persons Service which trains volunteer aides and helps to organize groups for discussion and mutual support. They apply Phyllis Silverman's preventive intervention principles.[4] Postponed repression of grief can cause other severe problems. Telephone reassurance networks are established and people are helped to develop new ways of coping and new relationships. AARP-RTA issues publications with notice of up-to-date programs, resources, travel opportunities and advice.

An example of another volunteer mutual help group is the SIDS Program. Sudden Infant Death Syndrome takes 20,000 infants each year. Parents who have lost an infant from an unknown cause are helping one another and also helping scientists study the unexplained cause. With new legislation last year, the Center for Disease Control is now researching this sad phenomenon with the task of finding a preventative remedy.

Several Mental Health Associations across the country are organizing seminars for professionals, volunteers and individuals dealing with death and dying. In Tucson, Arizona the Funeral Directors Association approached the Mental Health Association, whose clergy committee has conducted seminars in various parts of the state. A similar pattern emerged in North Dakota with the state Mental Health Association cooperating with the LPN Association, and the Continuing Education, Division of the State School of Social Service to reach the whole state. In Shawnee County, Kansas a seminar has triggered a similar pattern of continued requests. These voluntary groups are pooling resources to meet a widespread human need in a variety of combinations, creating a healthier climate for persons grief-stricken as we all are at some time in our lives.

The person who wants to help others over a difficult period as an individual volunteer may have a more difficult time finding someone to help. Just as we know there is high turnover and a tendency to short span of organization for self-help groups without staff, the volunteer alone may not sustain his efforts. He would be wise to find help to be helpful through the kinds of groups I have mentioned or through volunteer placement staff in Volunteer Bureaus or Voluntary Action Centers, the local Welfare Department or through nursing home or hospital Volunteer Directors. A new occupation is struggling for professional recognition. Volunteer Directors are prepared to counsel with volunteers to match their interests and abilities to assignments which require particular skills or characteristics.

Together with the volunteers, Volunteer Directors are working to dispel the myths which persist about volunteers. In medical settings volunteers have been accepted for many years in task oriented or fund-raising roles, but work with deep and meaningful relationships to patients has often been blocked by myths. I define a myth as a belief which may or may not be true, but a belief which determines behavior. Thus if a nurse or a local social worker believes volunteers should not be deeply involved with patients, relationships will not be allowed to develop. Experience has shown a high degree of self-fulfilling prophecy in myths about volunteers: people who trust them have reliable volunteers around. People who can't *really* delegate *real* responsibility to volunteers find them superficially committed and unreliable! The climate set for volunteers which anticipates teamwork with staff makes the difference. Paid staff can multiply their own effectiveness many times over with cooperative volunteers. But an investment of time and trust is essential for such dividends.

There are a few differences between paid staff and volunteers but almost every kind of person now can volunteer. No longer is volunteering limited to priveleged people, but it is an outlet for professionals, people employed at dull jobs as well as the mother whose young have left the nest. Each has a potential contribution

to make so that it is no longer a subordinate–superordinate relationship in either direction. We must plan backup staffing with volunteers, because they must usually have primary obligations which
take precedence over their volunteer work. We need to have substitutes ready when a volunteer is prevented from serving. Such
substitute jobs fall to experienced able persons who can fill in as
needed. This is a forum of recognition appreciated by volunteers.

A skilled Director of Volunteers will start with the rest of the
staff and executive support, identifying unmet needs and the kinds
of persons who might be recruited as volunteers. A volunteer should
have considerable orientation to the setting before taking on
thanatology roles. Most families of dying persons involved are far
too vulnerable to serve as the teachers, although the volunteer will
indeed learn a great deal from each experience. But there must be
someone, perhaps a more experienced volunteer if not a staff
member, who can help volunteers, dying persons and their families.
Our ordinary lives have too long been spent in avoidance of talk
about death and dying for us to be ready to cope without a lot of
reassurance and support. Not all persons will elect to volunteer in
thanatology roles, but some will, and we must make that possible.

Thus, in sequence the Director of Volunteer must develop good
relationships with the executive and the staff and involve them in
decisions about what volunteers could do, arranging for their
orientation to volunteers as well as thanatology theory before
defining volunteer assignments. We should consider assigning able
volunteers to a family situation, rather than to a task-defined
specific time slot. In situations involving dying persons, there are
innumerable things a volunteer could do as the situation changes,
and the volunteer must be flexible enough to vary schedules and
kinds of activities as the situation requires.

You will be hearing from the Red Cross Director of Volunteers
(who is a volunteer himself!) about the program at Walter Reed
Hospital in which the Red Cross aids in all sorts of ways, the families
of children who are terminally ill, from finding housing, to taking
other children in the family to the zoo. Such volunteers don't
worry about what their original job description said, but what seems
to be most needed which the paid staff cannot provide.

I especially point out this resource for attention to children in a family in which someone is terminally ill. It is difficult for such a child to be facing loss and feeling helpless, with other family members needing and getting more attention. It seems to me that some volunteers could carry out excursions for such children as well as counselling, or while the parents are getting advice, do something at the child's level, to lift him out of his situation for a while!

The Volunteer Director may become the person to whom the volunteer turns when the situation changes. Technically, the paid staff have no jurisdiction after a patient is no longer a patient, but volunteers can help to bridge the family to other sources of help in an ombudsman role. The Director of Volunteers has a wealth of information about community resources which the volunteer can relay to the family.

Working toward this institute has been a growth experience for me. How reassuring it has been to find so many people working to ease others over one of life's most difficult phases, its ending. Although I have lived long enough to come to believe there are many life experiences worse than death, I have also come to understand how dealing with death dwarfs many other problems and gives persons a different perspective, different values, and different resources. We are fortunate to live in times when death and dying can be openly discussed. I have felt anguish for my friends who still cannot face it. I believe offering opportunities to volunteers to serve in this area rounds out the full spectrum of volunteer choices.

To make this activity possible, we must arrange to support volunteers in this field with orientation, training and someone wise to turn to as they learn. To be entrusted with these kinds of responsibilities is recognition in itself, but we must be ever watchful for the opportunity to express appreciation on behalf of those who may not be able to express it—not just with pins or certificates at the end of the year, but a special word from the other staff who observe the contribution the volunteer has made, and communicate respect for the kind of person who could take on this kind of service.

Two news items have recognized one commercial business capitalizing on the needs we shall be discussing. In Time last February 19 an article reported on Theshold "a new Los Angeles business that has trained and will supply death companions to help ease lonely dying clients out of the world. The cost: $7.50 an hour of which the companion keeps $3.50——There may be more services to come . . . 'Dying is spectacular,' says Roberts (who started the business) I've even thought of making some kind of production out of it—like having the Mormon Tabernacle Choir come sing at your bedside if you could afford it." Rather than blame anyone for such crass commercialism, let's acknowledge the vacuum which exists.

Nicholas Von Hofman in the Washington Post of September 18 headlined *Morbidity Practiced Here* wonders if Medicare or Blue Cross will reimburse for the Los Angeles Threshold service, where the "Thanatologist" will rank in the medical hierarchy, and points out how other professions will be able to abdicate responsibility to the Thanatologist, and "they take a great burden off the small nuclear family." Such commercialism is horrifying, but could only happen if there is a real need being met. Los Angeles also has a volunteer counselling service for the dying and their families. A 24-hour telephone number has volunteers on call to answer questions or make personal visits in a project called "Shanti" from the Hindu word that translates as "the peace that passes understanding," according to Dr. Charles Garfield of UCLA who has mobilized 300 volunteers, 60% of whom are professional social workers, psychologists, nurses, clergymen.[5] It is my hope that as they usually do, other volunteers with strength, idealism and altruism will offer to meet this need elsewhere, that our institutions will make it possible through underwriting costs and supporting them emotionally as they serve this universal human need to face the realities of death and its implications for all the persons involved.

Footnotes

1. ACTION - Census Bureau 1974 Study.

2. Heard on the "Not for Women Only" TV show on Voluntarism, May 1975.

3. Robert Fulton, "The Widow in America: Some Sociological Observations" in Phyllis Silverman, ed., *The Widow to Widow* Program (New York, Health Sciences Publishing Corp.)

4. Phyllis Silverman, Widowhood and Preventive Intervention.

5. N.Y. Times August 17, 1975.

27

Myths: Barrier Beliefs About Volunteering

"Volunteer program" is a misnomer: volunteers are resource people to be matched to needs in an overall program. Counselling, orientation training and recognition help them work in concert with paid staff at every level from Executive/Board Chairman teams to Case Worker/Case Aide partnership. A volunteer development system makes volunteers a part of the overall program system.

Many barriers to the development of volunteer potential are myths, beliefs which determine actions whether or not they happen to be true. A myth can make or break the intent of a volunteer to serve or convince an agency not to use voluntary resources. There is just enough truth in myths about volunteers to perpetuate stereotypes and make the job of a volunteer coordinator or director much more difficult than it needs to be. For example, "most volunteers are women" may turn off men. Yet 41% in 1974 were men, according to the ACTION-Census Bureau study showing an increase from 21 million in 1965 to 38 million in 1974.

"Government, business, and voluntarism are separate independent sectors in the human services fields," whereas they are deeply interlocked and interdependent. By law and in practice, both voluntary organizations and businesses get grants, fees and contracts for purchase of service paid by tax funds. But profit makers can even lobby and write it off as a business expense, while voluntary agencies are not allowed to use a "substantial part" of their resources to improve legislation. Self-interested or profit groups are able to lobby free, while altruists have to pay dearly for influencing legislation and public opinion!

"Everyone is for volunteering, like motherhood and apple pie."
Lip-service level commitment, however, sometimes masks fear,
distrust or false assumptions. Fear was seldom openly articulated
until recently when volunteers began to be seen as a real threat to
paid staff in the present shrinking labor market.

The National Organization for Women has pointed out, with
echoes from some leaders of the labor movement and a sprinkling
of economists, that some volunteers do things that ought to be paid
work, thus depressing the labor market, particularly entry level jobs
for marginally employable people. A primary principle of the
volunteer development system is that volunteers supplement but
don't supplant paid positions. Actually, volunteering is often a route
toward employability.

Many governmental and profit making human services are
recruiting volunteers to extend and reinforce paid staff work.
Volunteers here as in voluntary agencies and self-help groups are
sometimes highly qualified persons whom we could never afford
for the special services they render for free. This has perpetuated the
myth that volunteers are "free labor" which is not true. It costs a real
investment to get and to keep volunteers, but it is an investment in
support for service which can pay high dividends in the long run by
preventing crises and chronicity which would require much more
expensive forms of care, such as institutionalization, expensive in
money and in dehumanizing persons.

"Volunteers can do anything paid staff do." We know from a
few isolated studies, that some former volunteers are working in
paid jobs which they created and demonstrated effectiveness originally as volunteers. Almost all of the human services were invented
by volunteers. As needs multiplied, work became more complex and
demanding of time, so it became paid work, even a profession, as
in social work, recreation therapy, etc. We believe that volunteers
have unique relationships to people and an imaginative perception
of human needs which means that they have created more paid
opportunities than they ever blocked. But they make a limited time
commitment, and necessarily have another source of income which
is likely to carry primary obligations which transcend those to
volunteering. (To family, profession, employers, etc.) In spite of the
recent ACTION Census Bureau findings that only 2% of the

Americans who volunteer are hoping for paid employment, the myth persists that volunteers may take away paid jobs.

Another real fear has been that volunteers will scrutinize programs with a critical eye, and embarrass the paid staff. A hospital superintendent once told me, "I'm not sure we need any spies around here." I have often wondered what it was he feared having discovered. Other executives have said, "I don't need to worry about that part of our program where there are volunteers in and out every day. They keep us all on our toes." In actual practice, volunteers more often become active advocates for the services in which they are involved: for better support, for higher pay for the staff, and they mobilize program resources.

A particularly destructive myth is that volunteer time is worth less than time of paid staff. Both, like all the rest of us, get exactly the same amount, 24 hours a day. But somehow in the eight-hour day of a paid job, a worker seldom has enough time to accomplish all he would like to do. But a volunteer offers his discretionary time for service or administrative responsibilities. This should be regarded as *more* valuable than paid staff time, and often the beneficiaries of volunteer services feel that way about it. But somehow with no hourly wage, we often see volunteers waiting around while paid staff do something "more important." If at the outset we see this gift of time as valuable, as it really is, we will maximize the use of it instead of feeling subjectively that it really isn't very important because we aren't paying for it by the hour.

Another myth to be dispelled is that "volunteers can't be evaluated or fired." Volunteers, like paid staff, want to do a good job. They want to be told *what is a good job*! Praise for poor work or overdone for small efforts destroys credibility. *Real* evaluation with the volunteer can be the most important recognition to that volunteer's development. When he discovers he is misplaced or overburdened a volunteer should feel free to say so. A volunteer development system regularizes a periodic review, counselling everyone, meaning promotion time for some or release for others without loss of face. Horizontal as well as upward mobility revitalizes volunteers as well as paid staff. We are abusing volunteers when we leave them too long in one spot without encouraging them to make a change to broaden their understanding of the whole program.

Of course, there are some unreliable people; some may be volunteers, some paid staff. But there is self-fulfilling prophecy in the way people react to expectations. Volunteers are not different from paid staff: once they understand the reason for confidentiality, or why people rely on them, they can be counted on, or they screen themselves out.

Many myths surround the training of volunteers, the most difficult to dispel being the illusion that there are "trained" volunteers who know everything, "somewhere there is *one* right answer to every question, one rule or recipe which 'they' know'". People seek certainty in a changing world, and unfortunately there isn't as much as we would like. Unlearning beliefs is the hardest part of learning, but fortunately old dogs *can* learn new tricks, for the truth does change!

Leaders emerge from the crucible of experience—they are not born, but made, and training makes a good many people into leaders with confidence based in the new competencies they learned as volunteers. There is a period of grace at the beginning of a job where you can ask all sorts of questions, but after that ends, you are supposed to *know*. It becomes embarrassing to ask. That's why it is important to offer frequent consultation, round tables, or other learning opportunities, where people can test their knowledge without risk. The myth of "trained" volunteer persists, but one briefing doesn't do it. Training can take all forms, any methods, all kinds of techniques, all kinds of groupings, but the important factor is continuing learning. We never know when we are going to need a new skill or technology, or have a new problem to solve.

Job descriptions have their place, particularly as people begin work, or review it in evaluating past experience, but they can become constraints instead of enabling. They have created a false dichotomy between service and policy volunteers. The myth we are beginning to crack is that one job description will fit many persons or last a long time. Ellen Straus, President of Call for Action, has been advocating individual contracts which can be changed whenever the need arises. People grow, their commitment increases, their interests change as volunteers as well as in paid work. If 65% of Americans don't like their paid jobs, as the HEW study *Work in America* stated, some of them are going to seek the missing satisfactions from volunteering. Let them find relationships, clarity of purpose and a sense of worth in their volunteer work, and we will have less turnover in volunteering than in the market place. Both have been running about ⅓ dropout in the first year, in some industries more. Yet we still have the myth that the "volunteer is here today and gone tomorrow!"

Volunteers take a dim view of the way services are delivered in some places where agencies concentrate on what they do *not* do instead of what they could. Particularly, there is a mystique surrounding helping professions, and research, and many volunteers don't realize what a vital role they could play in building a body of solid knowledge about human services and delivery patterns. Because their wisdom, if they happen not to be professionals of one sort or another, is non-technical, they are blocked from participating in research. Yet their observations are accurate, not self-interested, and potentially very valuable perspectives on the impact of services. They even have good ideas about "receiving systems" to fit "delivery systems" but because they are not part of the regular staff, they often are blocked from participating in planning and policy decisions. The tragedy is that it is the recipients of services who are the losers—and often they could make the most realistic, sensitized and authentic volunteers themselves. Too bad they are seldom asked! With a volunteer development system, volunteering can be a route into employability.

Experts worry about the fragmentation of families, and even of individuals who need a variety of highly specialized services. As opportunities come along to participate in health planning and resource development, volunteers can bridge persons between services, and from their experiences learn enough to be among the consumer majority required by law. Under Title XX, 1974 Social Services Amendments, volunteers have valuable suggestions to offer, just as they do in planning education, rehabilitation and mental health services, too.
development.

In direct service roles they can provide linkages if the agencies will allow them to work on behalf of an individual or a family, instead of on a circumscribed "job". The myth of "our" volunteers has got to go. If we free volunteers to move along with a family from a preventive service to a rehabilitation one, from crisis intervention to follow-up we will have them recycle, return to us freely when they are ready. By possessiveness, agencies lose volunteers who do not like being required to be loyal to an organization instead of to people in need.

The most pervasive myth of all is fragmentation of volunteer development by fields of service: "It takes a teacher for school volunteers, a social worker for social services or a probation officer in corrections to manage the matching of volunteers to beneficiaries of volunteer services." Newcomers to the field are proving otherwise. Volunteer Directors come from all sorts of backgrounds including experience as volunteers themselves, which is now counted by Civil Service. Many are coming from organized religion. The crucial characteristics are integrity, warmth, enthusiasm, caring, as well as skills in the management process. With the tremendous legislative push to organize planning groups, advisory committees and "lay" boards, informed, experienced volunteers are the best equipped citizens for these roles. They participate as generalists to balance the compulsions of the specialists and to speak for those they know and care about, who cannot speak for themselves.

Most myths are man-made and can be overcome. Accomplishing goals through the efforts of other people is what program administration is all about. Some of the people should be volunteers, who bring enthusiasm, compassion and energy when they offer their time. These qualities are hard to maintain against lack of faith, but with support they make a great difference toward meeting human needs with or without technical skills to help people. Warmth and concern are often more meaningful than technical skills in helping people. Technicians focus on the problem, but volunteers focus on the person. Our society has few outlets for compassion and greater needs for it now than ever. The more caring we channel into human services, the more fruitful those services can be. Professions can make this claim, but we make it especially for volunteer person-power.

There is a myth which some staff want to believe, started by David Sills in his study of the National Foundation and stressed in the 1968 Inaugural Address that volunteers don't care about policy making, only "small, splendid efforts." Fortunately, volunteers are like staff: when they see a need and feel powerless, they seek ways to meet it. Boards, advisory committees, evaluation teams all need a leavening of volunteers who care, without self-interest, along with consumers constrained by their needs and the paid staff and professionals with personal job requirements. We can't really overcome the impact of inflation and depression but with a volunteer development system we can bring in volunteer caring and concerns to undergird the program system, and then free them to turn public policy priorities toward unmet needs.

Volunteers can make the difference!

28

A Volunteer Development System

One out of every four Americans over the age of 13 does some form of volunteer work during the year. That means that nearly 40 million citizens—40 percent of whom are men—give their time, energy, and effort to some cause.

This vast resource is often untapped by human services delivery systems supported by HEW. Although administrators of human services programs universally express commitment to greater volunteer participation, and often volunteer themselves, few take full advantage of this valuable potential. Inadequate planning for volunteer participation is generally the reason for lack of meaningful volunteer involvement.

HEW encourages volunteering because:

* Volunteering as an option is a basic human right—everyone can help someone. We all need to be needed.

* Volunteers can represent a significant program resource, and they can provide a capacity to mobilize community support.

* Volunteers can extend and reinforce the work of paid staff—but they should never be used to supplant paid staff.

* Volunteers can improve program performance by acting as linkages within the community, interpreters of services, advocates for the inarticulate, as recuiters, trainers, or super-visors, and extend the outreach of the paid staff in delivering services.

* Volunteers come from all parts of communities, are all ages and do all sorts of things. Never underestimate the value of youth, older persons, the poor, or minorities to improve the quality of programs.

In order to use their abilities effectively and to grow, volunteers need help. This should be in the form of a well-planned volunteer development system based on the following principles:

1. A freedom of choice is essential for volunteers, staff, and the person being served. Volunteers work *with*, not for other people. Expectations and goals should be defined in clear, contractural terms.
2. Volunteers need appropriate placement to utilize their skills, knowledge, and interests; training to supplement their knowledge and skills; a place and tools to work with; and someone to turn to for support, encouragement, and appreciation.
3. Volunteers need periodic review of their accomplishments and growth opportunities when ready for more or different responsibilities; records to prove their service and training; and recognition.
4. Volunteers need access to the policy development process. Firsthand perspective helps policy makers focus on priority needs.

A volunteer development system produces enriched and more effective services and an informed dedicated citizenry ready to participate in collaborative efforts outside the agency in meeting human needs, and attacking problems. Solving some problems may create new ones, so there is an ever-expanding need for this kind of citizen network.

A volunteer system must be well conceived and create a climate in which people can risk giving their best. An ideal program is staffed with a full-time administrator who decentralizes administration to line staff as readiness is indicated.

Provision of opportunities to participate in policy development, program innovation, and advocacy roles attracts and motivates the best volunteers. A volunteer system is a continuously intrinsic part of the overall program planning cycle and fits into the total system, rather than being a separate program.

All long-range planning in the human services delivery area should include explicit provisions for volunteer participation in providing services, in interpretation, setting program goals, and in carrying out program goals.

The following chart illustrates the basic elements of a volunteer development system. Additional information can be obtained by writing Office of Volunteer Development, HEW, Washington, D.C. 20201.

SERVICES		VOLUNTEERS	YOUTH	COLLEGE STUDENTS	HOUSEWIVES	PROFESSIONAL PERSONS	EMPLOYED PERSONS	AGING PERSONS (60+)	MALE	FEMALE	CONSUMERS	TOTAL
SERVICES TO ORGANIZATIONS	#											
	HRS											
CARETAKING	#											
	HRS											
STAFF ASSISTANT	#											
	HRS											
SOCIAL SUPPORT	#											
	HRS											
BRIDGING	#											
	HRS											
ADVOCATE	#											
	HRS											
SPECIAL SKILLS AS	#											
	HRS											
1. Arts 2. Music	#											
	HRS											
3. Ecology 4. Public Relations	#											
	HRS											
5. Educational	#											
	HRS											
COMMUNITY REPRESENTATIVES	#											
	HRS											
1. Minority Groups	#											
	HRS											
2. Youth	#											
	HRS											
3. Geographic Section	#											
	HRS											
4. Aging	#											
	HRS											
5. Consumers	#											
	HRS											
TOTAL	#											
	HRS											
%												

PHASE III—EVALUATION/FUTURE PLANNING

Executive	Volunteer Director	Unit Line Staff and Supervisors
A. Evaluate actual performance of the volunteer development system against targeted goals and objectives	A. Collate and record volunteer service and training	A. Evaluate impact of volunteer effort on: Staff Target group (consumers) Volunteers
B. Assess overall effect of volunteer on agency's ability to respond to needs	B. Assess referrals, dropouts, special accomplishments, services; consumer, volunteer, and community reactions	B. Assess performance of executive and Volunteer Director in the volunteer development system
C. Assess overall cost/benefit of volunteer development system	C. Assess the capacity of volunteers to provide services and accept responsibilities through staff, consumer, and community reactions; honors; offices held; etc.	C. Summarize and make recommendations of program effectiveness from staff reports, target group responses, volunteer assessment
D. Assess long-range effects of volunteer development system on agency consumers, community	D. Assess effects of volunteer development system on community understanding	D. Submit plans for supervision patterns and on-the-job training
E. Provide for volunteer perspective input in new program development cycle	E. Measure impact of volunteer effort on program operations/delivery of services	E. Submit future requests for volunteers, suggest sources
F. Makes recommendations for future priorities for volunteer development system	F. Summarize and make recommendations from data gathered for future priorities for volunteer development system	
G. Recognize the status of Volunteer Director as member of top administrative team and volunteers as essential to agency services	G. Adjust recruiting, referral and training plans in tune with new priorities	
	H. Insure volunteer perspective in future program development efforts	

PHASE I—PREPARATION

Executive	Volunteer Director or Coordinator	Line Staff and Supervisors
Demonstrate support for volunteer development:	Define goals and objectives for volunteer development system:	A. Define unit and specific program objectives for volunteer services, unmet needs, volunteer opportunities, requirements
A. Establish volunteer development system	A. Work with unit heads, line staff representative volunteers, and consumers defining needs for volunteers	B. Contribute ideas for volunteer assignments, group projects
B. Set long-range goals and objectives for volunteer development system involving leadership, paid staff, boards, or committees, volunteers, and consumers	B. Assess community for volunteer resources:	C. Suggest ways target group members could volunteer

C. Appoint qualified Director to focus efforts	1. Volunteers
	      Voluntary Action Center
	      Service Groups
	      Schools and colleges, etc.
		D. Schedule time for:

D. Designate staff time to define roles, prepare training, evaluate plans, meetings	2. Organizations interested in cooperation	1. Own training
E. Communicate support through:	C. Establish referral, reporting, and record systems	2. Counseling, placing, working with and through volunteers

Staff meetings
   Memos of authorization
   Public statements
	D. Plan and budget for:	3. Participation in orientation and training of volunteers

	Office services
	   Volunteer expenses
	   Public relations
	   Recognition process
		4. Unit staff meetings, volunteer meetings, joint staff/volunteer meetings

	E. Develop orientation and training procedures for:
	   Staff
	   Volunteers
	   Self
		5. Recording and reporting quantity, quality, impact

PHASE II–OPERATION

Executive	Volunteer Director	Unit Line Staff and Supervisors
A. Support recruitment through public statements, community activities	A. Activate continuous targeted recruiting	A. Interview, place volunteers
B. Offer explicit encouragement—welcome trainees	B. Develop skill bank and record bank of opportunities for volunteer assignments	B. Refer target group members as volunteers
C. Monitor progress	C. Counsel new volunteers, refer to units	C. Recruit volunteers from own professional groups, membership organizations
D. Informal observation	D. Operate orientation, training events	D. Operate on-the-job training for volunteers, provide counseling or supervision in groups as well as to individuals
E. Encourage staff cooperation	E. Record assignments, training	E. Review impact and extent of volunteer participation in unit
F. Allocate support as needed	F. Participate in program development	F. Provide regular reports of service, changes, new needs, training requests, program recommendations
	G. Cooperate with other agencies, educators to develop learning opportunities and joint programming	G. Participate in recognition process—selection, awards, promotion to greater responsibilities, etc.
	H. Operate feedback system through meetings, roundtables, evaluations	H. Provide feedback from experience for future planning, public education, citizen recruitment
	I. Represent volunteerism—to executive, staff, consumers, volunteers, volunteer resource groups, public	
	J. Arrange for mobility and progression of volunteers; recognition of volunteers, staff	
	K. Work with community volunteer administrators, professional volunteer centers, civic and consumer groups	

WHO DOES WHAT FOR VOLUNTEER SERVICES
CYCLE OF PROGRESS

	Volunteer Coordinator or Director of Volunteers	**Agency Supervisor of Volunteer Service in Program**
Work Analysis	Establish Executive and staff support of need for Volunteer Services to carry out program goals and translate tasks into assignments for individual and group volunteers.	Find things volunteers could do to help, time and qualities required, job descriptions for entry jobs and promotion routes.
Promotion And Recruitment	Use all available media to describe opportunities to groups and individuals in community. Interview and refer volunteers appropriately.	In the community encourage volunteering for your agency and refer volunteers to coordinator for initial choices and recording of interests.
Counselling	Continuous process: matching volunteer interests and available time to needs, offering choices to volunteers.	See referred volunteers, test suitability to job requirements, assign to staff who will supervise them there or refer back to coordinator.
Standards And Orientation	Describe background and program of agency, policies and standards to volunteers.	Introduce site ground rules, expectations about volunteers, needs of people being served, schedule, duties.
Training And Supervision	Plan with volunteers and staff continuing periodic events to train volunteers in groups, new films in field and round tables and volunteer feedback.	Give on-the-job supervision, involve volunteers in planning what they need to learn next, report staff and volunteer training needs to vol. coordinator.
Records And Reports	Keep records of volunteer services by groups and individual volunteers; tailor information for Executive, and general public, volunteers as individuals.	Document services given, differences volunteers make, project future needs for volunteers for Coordinator.
Periodic Evaluations	Review assignments with staff and volunteers, and community for potential volunteers and services. Cite unmet needs, new opportunities.	With volunteers, appraise their work, plan for future utilization of skills, time and resources, inform Coordinator of changes and training needed.
Recognition	Establish standards for service awards, plan and operate recognition process, develop promotion opportunities for new program goals.	Report benefits and human interest stories about volunteer services, opportunities for personal growth through varied and more complex assignments, promotion or release to Coordinator.

Future Shock by Toffler v
(retired volunteers)

N

J